# · CELTIC ·
# · PILGRIMAGES ·

## SITES, SEASONS AND SAINTS

*An Inspiration for Spiritual Journeys*

ELAINE GILL and DAVID EVERETT

Illustrated by
COURTNEY DAVIS

BLANDFORD

A BLANDFORD BOOK
First published in the UK 1997 by Blandford
A Cassell Imprint

CASSELL PLC
Wellington House
125 Strand
London WC2R 0BB

Distributed in the United States by Sterling Publishing Co., Inc.
387 Park Avenue South, New York, NY 10016–8810

**British Library Cataloguing-in-Publication Data**
A catalogue entry for this title is available from
the British Library

ISBN 0 7137 26431

Printed and bound by Wing King Tong Co., Hong Kong

# CONTENTS

# ACKNOWLEDGEMENTS

The editors and publishers have made every effort to contact copyright holders whose work is included in this book; however, omissions may inadvertently have occurred, and they will be pleased to hear from any copyright holder whose work is not properly acknowledged below.

**David Adam**: prayer from *The Cry of the Deer*;
**A. M. Allchin**: prayer about Pennant Melangell;
**Glenda Beagan**: 'They call me a saint';
**The Venerable Bede**: extract from A *History of the English Church and People*. Translated by Leo Sherley-Price.
© Leo Sherley-Price, 1955. Reproduced by kind permission of Penguin Books Ltd;
**Ciaran Brennan**: 'Skellig';
**D. M. and E. M. Lloyd**: extract from A *Book of Wales*. Collins 1953;
**Murdoch Maclean**: 'Trim the cruisie's failing light'. By kind permission of the Iona Community;
**G. R. D. McLean**: extracts from *Poems of the Western Highlanders*, SPCK 1961;
**Kuno Meyer**: translated extracts from *Ancient Irish Poetry*. By kind permission of Constable and Company, Publishers;
**Extracts from the *Carmina Gadelica***: By kind permission of the Trustees of the Scottish Academic Press;
**Extracts from *Druidic Triads: The Wisdom of the Cymry***. By kind permission of the Holmes Publishing Group, USA;
**Extracts from the New International Version of the Bible**: International Bible Society.

Spiral of Life, based on *The Book of Kells*.

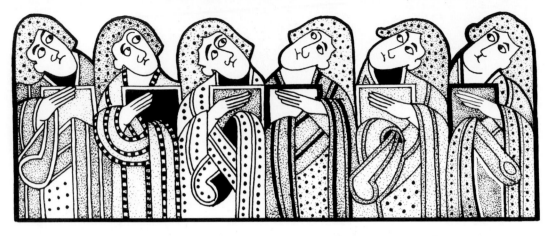

# INTRODUCTION

*I*T SEEMS that the Celtic tradition is speaking afresh to the hearts, minds and souls of many people today as they struggle for meaning and a sense of purpose in their lives. In a world that often appears confused and dark, and filled with hunger, strife and poverty, the simplicity and example of the Celtic saints and the deep peace of the sacred places associated with them touch something very profound in us and perhaps offer an anchor of sanity amid the chaos.

A life which did not encompass the spiritual was, and is, foreign to the Celtic nature and response to the world. Spirit suffuses matter, and the body and soul are knit together into a harmonious and balanced whole. There is no duality here, but rather a glorious celebration of life through which all is claimed and sanctified and is made whole.

Sometimes, however, we lose our balance. Life becomes distorted and out of kilter, the light is dim and disorder takes over. It is at these times that we need to step back, to take stock, and to reassess and reorientate ourselves. It is time to go on pilgrimage.

Pilgrimage is an evocative word with as many ideas as to what it might mean as there are people who stop to consider the concept, and in a sense we are all on a pilgrimage all of the time. It is usually a break from ordinary life and

spent in some sort of physical journey, unlike a retreat where one is based in one place and only the inward journey is undertaken. Each path is uniquely individual even if the same earthly route is followed, distance covered and experiences encountered, because we come to it as ourselves. We come from a past which has made us what we are and we start from where we are now, which makes us distinctive from our neighbour.

And so we set out with a specifically spiritual purpose. Maybe we have an objective in mind: perhaps to look for an answer or a new direction, or possibly just to wait on God and to make space and time to hear the still, small voice within.

What is pilgrimage but a journey of the soul, a labyrinth to tread towards self-discovery and knowledge of God? As mentioned above, this is often expressed in an outward journey which can be compared to the masculine solar

Wheel of Creation.

principle, but this needs to be balanced by the feminine lunar principle of the inner path. It is a time of spiritual passage, a place of change, a kind of death and rebirth. Perhaps we have outgrown old patterns and need to move into something new. Whatever the pilgrimage becomes for us, we do not finish our journey the same as when we started.

This book is a small offering to help you find a spirituality that speaks to you as you are. It is not intended as a guide for those who wish to have travel information, and so there are no timetables or tide-tables or details of accommodation; neither is it intended as a manual of spiritual exercises and direction. Rather, it is a starting point, a springboard and a companion for your own very personal journey. We hope that reading about these Celtic holy men and women and the places they inhabited will inspire you in the true sense of that word; that they may breathe new life into you and give you an impetus for your own pilgrimage, both inner and outer.

We hope that you will want to visit some of the sites mentioned in the text and that you will feel drawn to explore more fully the nature of the faith and beliefs of the Celtic saints who lived in these places. By doing this you will become a part of a living Celtic inheritance that is very much alive and is ours to embrace today.

In the Celtic legends there is always a sense of adventure into the unknown, with its attendant strands of growth and development. Alongside this is the strong consciousness of the sanctity of the land and of particular sites of power. These are also the themes of the Celtic pilgrim road.

You will notice that this book is divided into thirteen sections. Initially we had thought that it might be used by taking one chapter for each of the lunar months throughout the year, or alternatively by using one chapter per week for each of the thirteen weeks between the four major Celtic festivals of Samhain (1 November), Imbolc (1 February), Beltane (1 May) and Lughnasad (1 August), if one wished to cover the material more quickly. However, we are aware that today we have all but buried the lunar calendar in our modern world.

As we wish this book to be easily usable in a practical sense, and not too obscure, we have sacrificed some authenticity and kept to the twelve months of the more familiar Roman calendar, inserting the thirteenth month as a three-day period at the very end of October. This actually ties in with the thirteen calendar tree months of the Druids, who also used this three-day month at the end of their year. In this final section we have chosen to explore the theme of the Kingdom of Heaven, which is for Christians essentially the beginning and the end of all things.

The Calendar of Coligny, a metal disc dating from the first century BCE found near Lyons in 1897, shows how the Celts synchronized the lunar and the solar years, and so we hope we may be forgiven this compromise.

Pilgrimage can be both exciting and challenging, and is invariably rewarding, although maybe not in ways that we necessarily expect. Go with hope and courage and an open heart, and all will be well.

The Celtic Wheel of the Year showing the eight major fire festivals.

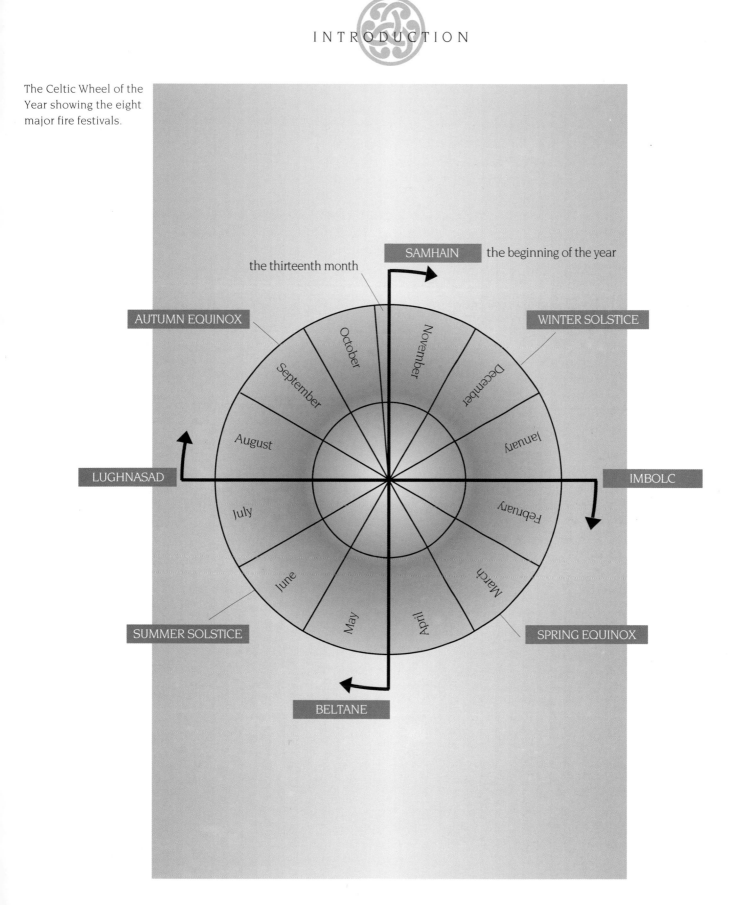

the thirteenth month

SAMHAIN   the beginning of the year

AUTUMN EQUINOX

WINTER SOLSTICE

LUGHNASAD

IMBOLC

SUMMER SOLSTICE

SPRING EQUINOX

BELTANE

October

November

September

December

August

January

July

February

June

March

May

April

*May the road rise to meet you.*
*May the wind be always at your back.*
*May the sun shine warm upon your face,*
*The rains fall soft upon your fields;*
*And until we meet again may*
*God hold you in the hollow of his hand.*

traditional Irish

May the saints be with you on your pilgrimage.

ELAINE GILL · DAVID EVERETT
Penzance, Cornwall/Kernow, 1996

Stone pillar with pilgrim from Ballyvourney, County Cork.

Stone with two pilgrim figures from Bressay, Shetland.

# N·O·V·E·M·B·E·R

**The Blessing of the New Year**

*God, bless to me the new day,*
*Never vouchsafed to me before;*
*It is to bless Thine own presence*
*Thou hast given me this time, O God.*

*Bless Thou to me mine eye,*
*May mine eye bless all it sees;*
*I will bless my neighbour,*
*May my neighbour bless me.*

*God, give me a clean heart,*
*Let me not from sight of Thine eye;*
*Bless to me my children and my wife,*
*And bless to me my means and my cattle.*

from the *Carmina Gadelica* (i,159)

*I*N OUR WESTERN WORLD the secular new year starts on 1 January, while in the Church calendar the first Sunday in Advent marks the beginning of the year. There are four Sundays during this time of preparation before the festival of Christmas, and so Advent Sunday can fall in either November or December, depending on the particular year. However, for the Celt, whether Christian or pagan, the transition to the new year starts at sunset on 31 October, which heralds the feast of Samhain, 1 November. As with the Jewish people, important days of celebration and the keeping of significant holy days always commence at dusk of the evening before and not at midnight.

At Samhain (pronounced "sow-ain") the setting of the sun on the last day of October marks the death of the old year and the following dawn the beginning of the new one. Thus for the ancient Celts the time between sunset and sunrise was considered to be very auspicious and somewhat dangerous, as the doors to the other worlds could be passed through very easily in this "time-between-times". On Samhain Eve in Ireland it was customary to weave a cross of wheat straw called a *parshell* and to place it inside over the doorway of the house, where it would remain as a protective sign for the coming year. This observance is repeated in the better-known custom of making St Bridget's Crosses at Imbolc on 1 February.

Samhain, or Hallowmas, is one of the four Celtic fire festivals which are spread throughout the year, the others being Imbolc (1 February), Beltane (1 May) and Lughnasad (1 August), and it may be named from the Gaelic *samh-f*

The four major Celtic fire festivals are Samhain, Imbolc, Beltane and Lughnasad.

*huin*, meaning "summer end". These four points of the year are intersected by the two solstices (December and June) and the two equinoxes (March and September).

It is thought that the significance of keeping 1 November and 1 May as two principal points in the cycle of the year owes its origin to the time when the Celts were mainly a pastoral people and dependent on their herds for sustenance. At Samhain, with the approach of winter, the animals would be brought in from their places of pasture to be nearer to the farmsteads, and those which were not needed for breeding in the coming year would be slaughtered and their flesh smoked or salted for the winter provisions. The theme of death is touched upon when the end of this seasonal cycle of growth and fertility is reached and the bleak days of winter begin. It is a time of uncertainty and confusion, when the declining power of the sun and the lengthening hours of darkness appear to dissolve the edges between the material and the spiritual worlds. For the Celts these two spheres were always closely interwoven and there was no clear division between the sacred and the secular. At certain times of the year the boundaries became even more blurred and the veil between the worlds appeared to be very thin, as at Samhain when the souls of the ancestors of the tribes were remembered. Stories of heroic deeds and tribal traditions were recounted as people gathered around their fires. Yet in the midst of this gloom and time of shadows is the promise of rebirth and new beginnings, the coming of a new year with its hopes and changes. It is a time of purification and for shedding old outmoded ways, while turning towards the future with new resolve.

Therefore November is a good month to start a pilgrimage. It is not the ideal month to go on a physical journey, for the weather is often foggy and the first frosts of winter arrive, but the onset of winter and the shift of emphasis to inside pastimes offer incentive and opportunity to undertake an inner journey. It is a time of remembrance, death and rebirth which encourages us to consider more serious and eternal matters. Also, it is a liminal time when we can pass through the gateway from the old to the new if we choose to do so.

In the Christian Church today, 1 November has become All Saints' Day, on which all the departed Christian saints, our spiritual ancestors, are remembered. The following day, 2 November, is All Souls' Day or All Hallows Day, when all the departed, and especially friends and relatives, are thought of with affection and mentioned in prayers by the Church. When the practice of the Roman Catholic Church superseded the Celtic calendar, these two days were superimposed on the old Celtic festival of Samhain and remain with us today.

This month we focus on Whithorn in south-west Scotland, in the region of Dumfries and Galloway, and on the two Celtic saints who are linked with this place: St Ninian, the Apostle to the Picts, and St Martin of Tours, whose feast day falls each year on 11 November.

Whithorn is said to be "the cradle of Christianity" in Scotland and visiting this small town today you will find three main sites associated with St Ninian.

The pilgrim.

Knotwork cross.

First, through a sixteenth-century archway in the main street are the ruins of the medieval priory, a church for the people, possibly standing on the site of the saint's earlier foundation. Here there is also a small museum housing a fine collection of stone crosses and monuments found in the local area. Secondly, about 2 miles to the south-east at the Isle of Whithorn, now joined to the mainland by a substantial causeway, is the roofless, thirteenth-century chapel where pilgrims from across the sea would have first come ashore and given thanks for their safe passage. One theory places Ninian's monastery and chapel on this site rather than in Whithorn. The third location is on the coast about 3 miles west of the Isle, down Physgill Glen. Here, at the far end of the stony beach, is Ninian's Cave where he used to come to spend times of retreat in solitude and prayer. There are early Christian crosses incised on the walls of the cave. An annual pilgrimage organized by the Roman Catholic Church is still made here each year during the summer. On the beach it is possible to find grey, sea-smoothed pebbles naturally marked with white quartz crosses, appropriate reminders of St Ninian's devotion.

This threefold pattern of sites was based on the ideas of St Martin of Tours, by whom Ninian was greatly influenced and inspired. Martin's father was a high-ranking officer in the Roman army and so his son was named after Mars, the Roman god of war, and the young man followed in his father's footsteps and became a Roman soldier himself. After becoming a Christian he wished to

*Opposite*:
Window of chapel at the Isle of Whithorn, vine-scroll decoration from the Ruthwell Cross and the entrance to St Ninian's Cave, Dumfries and Galloway.

turn from his military career and to spend time in prayer and service instead. Eventually he was made a bishop at Tours on the River Loire in Gaul, and his cathedral here corresponded to the church in Whithorn as a focus of worship for the local people. His monastic settlement was centred 1½ miles away at Marmoutier. Here about eighty monks lived in caves dug out of a cliff-face beside the river, meeting only for meals and corporate prayer. This was the equivalent of Ninian's monastery at the Isle of Whithorn.

As disciples flocked to Martin they became his *muinntir* or family and addressed him as "Papa", a word taken to Scotland by Ninian, and he exercised the same authority over them as the chief of a Celtic clan would have done. As more people joined the community it came to be called Mar-muinntir or Marmoutier, meaning "big family". Martin had an isolated place where he could withdraw privately for silence, and Ninian followed his example by choosing a cave on the seashore for this purpose. St Martin's Cross, a tall stone monument on the island of Iona, off the coast of Mull, is a further indication of how influential Martin's ideas were to the development of Celtic spirituality and monastic life.

The Celtic saints often favoured remote places for prayer and we shall see

St Ninian's Chapel at the Isle of Whithorn.

An early memorial stone at Whithorn recording "the place of Peter the Apostle".

further examples of this in the following chapters. They derived their inspiration not only from St Martin in Gaul but also from further afield in Egypt, where Christian hermits had withdrawn into the desert to live an austere life of poverty and prayer. These "Desert Fathers" were indeed the fathers of Western monasticism. Christianity had become the official religion of the Roman Empire after the emperor Constantine's Edict of Milan in 314 CE. This marked the end of persecution and martyrdom for Christians, but it also signalled the beginning of a period of corruption in the Christian Church, for with its new status came the pursuit of privilege and power.

The Desert Fathers in Egypt reacted against this development and in so doing inspired Celtic Christians in turn to withdraw to their own "deserts" or lonely places to preserve the purity and simplicity of their faith. St Antony and St Paul of Egypt were the most influential of these early holy men. It is noteworthy that the figure of St Antony is carved on the ancient Ruthwell Cross near Dumfries in south-west Scotland, on the tenth-century Penmon Cross in the priory on Anglesey, and also on the Cross of Muiredach at Monasterboice in Ireland, all indicating how far their ideas spread.

Our main sources of information about St Ninian are a Life written by the twelfth-century monk Ailred of Rievaulx, and a passage penned earlier by the Venerable Bede in *A History of the English Church and People*. It seems that he was born about 360 CE in Cumbria, possibly near St Patrick's later birthplace. He grew into a tall, strong young man and his father, a converted British chieftain, wanted him to become a soldier. However, Ninian had other plans and desired to be educated in the Christian faith, so he travelled to Rome, where at the age of twenty-one he was warmly welcomed by Pope Damasus. After several years of study, Pope Siricius ordained him and consecrated him as a bishop.

He returned to Britain to become a missionary to the southern Picts, who lived between the River Tay and the River Dee on the east coast of Scotland, and also to the people of Galloway in south-west Scotland. On his homeward journey he visited St Martin of Tours at Marmoutier, which, as we have seen, became a model for the monastic structure at Whithorn. In 396 CE, a few years before the Roman legions finally withdrew from Britain, the see of Whithorn was established. According to the Venerable Bede, writing about 300 years later, it was known as Candida Casa, meaning the White House or Shining Place. This may have been because the church was painted white or had distinctive white mortar between its stones, or because it became a beacon of spiritual light to the surrounding areas. In the Northumbrian language it was called Hwit Aerne, from which the current name of Whithorn is derived. The church was completed in 397 CE, about the time that St Martin died, and was dedicated to him, being known as Taigh Martin in Gaelic.

In Ireland, Candida Casa was known as the Great Monastery and Martin was held in special veneration by the early Irish church. A copy of *The Life of Martin of Tours* by Sulpicius Severus appears in *The Book of Armagh* and may date from as early as the fifth century, and at Nendrum on Island Mahee in

Strangford Lough, County Down, an early church was founded which was undoubtedly a daughter community of Candida Casa.

Altogether St Ninian's ministry lasted more than thirty-five years, until his death in September 432 CE. He was buried at Whithorn and consequently the town became a very important centre of pilgrimage, rivalling Santiago de Compostela in Spain, with people coming from as far afield as France, Spain and Prussia to visit his tomb. On the Tuesday of Whitsun week St Ninian's relics used to be carried in solemn procession and as many as 10,000 people would gather for the occasion. The fame of Whithorn spread throughout Europe, and Alcuin, an English scholar at the court of Charlemagne, sent gifts to the shrine. In 1501 King James IV gave a silver reliquary to contain the arm-bone of the saint. Many other royal personages also journeyed to Whithorn: in 1329 King Robert the Bruce came seeking a cure of his leprosy and later his son King David II also came for healing. King James IV was the most regular royal pilgrim, making the journey eight times. The only known surviving fragment of a relic of Ninian is that contained in a small, twelfth-century reliquary now in the British Museum.

In 1581 there was an Act of Parliament prohibiting pilgrimages, as these were considered to promote idolatry, and so Whithorn, like many other places, declined from its former glory. Thankfully, in recent years the Whithorn Trust, with their excellent archaeological work, are making Ninian and his followers known again not only in Galloway, where he has never really been forgotten, but also in the wider Church. Each year on or near St Ninian's feast day in September the Whithorn Lecture, about the historic and religious background of the site, is given in the town.

The chosen poverty and simplicity of the Celtic saints were among their most distinctive features, and once again Martin of Tours was influential in this. While still a Roman soldier in Amiens in northern Gaul, he cut his military cloak in half and gave part of it to a needy beggar. This act of charity has inspired many works of art in which Martin is seen, usually on a horse, offering half his cloak to the poor man. Later that night Martin had a vision in which he saw Jesus wearing that portion of the garment he had given to the beggar.

I needed clothes and you clothed me.

Gospel of St Matthew (ch. 25, v. 36)

The spirit of St Martin lives on today in work done by such places as the Crypt of St Martin-in-the-Fields in central London, where the poor are cared for in a very practical way by being fed and clothed.

The monastic communities started by Martin at Tours and by Ninian at Whithorn were like families, where possessions were held in common. In this sense these communities copied the first groups of Christians in Jerusalem, who handed over their possessions to a common purse which was then used for the benefit of all and the relief of poverty.

However, the poverty of the communities at Tours and Whithorn, and earlier in Jerusalem, was not simply about lack of possessions. By their lifestyle they displayed the value of chosen spiritual poverty in which they turned their backs on the pursuit of status, power and riches, and gave their lives to the service of God and his creation.

The inner journey this month therefore encourages us to pursue "poverty of spirit" and a new way of life. In our human state, this is not something which comes easily or naturally to us. Like any pilgrimage, it can be a long and arduous struggle during which the destination seems to be a long way off. It is not simply a question of renouncing material possessions, which in turn can lead to an attitude of spiritual arrogance and self-satisfaction, but of recognizing one's own poor spiritual condition and need of God.

> Blessed are the poor in spirit, for theirs is the kingdom of heaven.
>
> Gospel of St Matthew (ch. 5, v. 3)

Even suffering or struggling does not necessarily bring us closer to God. We suffer because we cut ourselves off from the divine source and deny God access to our innermost being. However, this often serves the purpose of showing us our own depth of need, our poverty of spirit. Once we have been brought low and made to recognize our need of God, hopefully we can once again go forward on the pilgrim path in all humility.

Before setting out on any journey, it is usual to make preparations and these are equally important for an inner pilgrimage. There can be just as many potential hazards, pitfalls and dangers on the inner journey as on any trek across a desert or mountain wasteland, and it would be foolish not to anticipate such trials. As a soldier-saint, Martin can be a timely reminder of how we need to be properly protected and to equip ourselves for the journey ahead.

> Finally, be strong in the Lord and in the strength of his might. Put on
> the whole armour of God, that you may be able to stand against the
> wiles of the devil. Stand therefore, having girded your loins with
> truth, and having put on the breastplate of righteousness, and
> having shod your feet with the equipment of the gospel of peace;
> above all taking the shield of faith, with which you can quench all
> the flaming darts of the evil one. And take the helmet of salvation
> and the sword of the Spirit, which is the word of God.
>
> St Paul's Letter to the Ephesians (ch. 6, vv. 10, 11, 14–17)

A time of quiet prayer or meditation each morning on rising and each evening before sleep is the ideal, but don't worry if you can't spend very long; time is about depth not length. If you are unable to do this, then at least throw

a *caim* about yourself and ask for protection and guidance. The following story explains well the nature of the *caim* – that is, a circle of protection – and how powerful it can be.

At a certain time each year it was St Ninian's habit to bless the flocks and herds which grazed on the land attached to the priory, and for this purpose the animals were gathered together in one place. The saint marked out on the ground with his staff a *caim* around the cattle. Darkness fell before they could be returned to their pasture and during the night a band of thieves came and, finding the beasts unattended, had the idea of driving them away. The cattle panicked and in the ensuing chaos the head robber was gored to death by a bull. At this the other thieves were filled with fear and sought to flee, but they were unable to penetrate the invisible wall created by the protective circle. Hearing shouts and cries, Ninian rushed to find out the cause of the disturbance and, having compassion on the men in their plight, prayed that the dead man might be whole once more and brought back to life. Then he blessed the repentant thieves and let them go on their way.

We can invoke this same protection in a spiritual way for ourselves each day. Casting a *caim* is a technique that was used by Christian Celts, both Protestant and Roman Catholic, and it is still valid. Draw an invisible circle around yourself with your right index finger by extending your arm towards the ground and turning clockwise with the sun. As you do this, become aware that you are safe and encompassed by the love of God: that you are encircled, enfolded and protected.

*Circle me Lord*
*Keep protection near*
*And danger afar*

*Circle me Lord*
*Keep hope within*
*Keep doubt without*

*Circle me Lord*
*Keep light near*
*And darkness afar*

*Circle me Lord*
*Keep peace within*
*Keep evil out*

contemporary Celtic
prayer by David Adam

# D·E·C·E·M·B·E·R

*A time ere came the Son of God,*
  *The earth was a black morass,*
*Without star, without sun, without moon,*
  *Without body, without heart, without form.*

*Illumined plains, illumined hills,*
  *Illumined the great green sea,*
*Illumined the whole globe together,*
  *When the Son of God came to earth.*

from the *Carmina Gadelica* (ii, 173)

*D*ECEMBER is the darkest time of the year for those of us who live in the northern hemisphere, and is the month when the sun is at its furthest point, resulting in the shortest day and long hours of darkness. Yet as the wheel of the year turns, this is, perhaps surprisingly, when the Celt celebrates the return of the light and its growing strength, for the instant the sun enters the zodiacal sign of Capricorn at the winter solstice a few days before Christmas, it begins its return journey northwards and is moving towards its full power at the summer solstice six months later in June.

People rejoice in the waxing light of the physical sun at this time of the year, and Celtic Christians also welcome the birth of light of a spiritual nature in the incarnation of the Christ-child.

The Word became flesh and made his dwelling among us. We have

seen his glory, the glory of the One and Only, who came from the Father, full of grace and truth.

Gospel of St John (ch. 1, v. 14)

There is a tradition in the Western Isles of Scotland that St Bridget, or St Bride as she is sometimes known, was present in the stable at Bethlehem at the birth of Jesus and acted as aid-woman, or midwife, to Mary. She is also called the foster-mother of Christ, and she is the patroness of spring and birth. Her own feast day falls at Imbolc, the time when the sheep bore their lambs and came into milk. During labour, women in Uist would call on her for help when giving birth to their own children.

*There came to me assistance,*
*Mary fair and Bride;*
*As Anna bore Mary,*
*As Mary bore Christ,*
*As Eile bore John the Baptist*
*Without flaw in him,*
*Aid thou me in mine unbearing,*
*    Aid me, O Bride!*

from the Carmina Gadelica (i, 177)

In this way they linked themselves to the cosmic event that took place in Palestine 2,000 years ago, and by identifying with the divine they merged the physical and spiritual worlds, a process which comes so easily to the Celtic temperament.

Like many ancient peoples, the Celts passed their knowledge and wisdom from one generation to another by word of mouth. The Druids were the custodians of their oral tradition and esoteric knowledge, and it took as long as twenty years to be fully trained in the customs, laws, religion and poetry of their society.

Many of the Christian teachings accepted by the Celts were strikingly similar to the earlier Druidic ones, and in some places it was with relative ease that the two traditions were enmeshed. Indeed, Pope Gregory I issued a papal bull encouraging this blending of the two strands. British Druids were clairvoyantly aware of the birth of Jesus Christ and of his subsequent Crucifixion. One legend tells how they sent their most precious cup to Jerusalem to be used at the Last Supper, and how it was returned by Joseph of Arimathea when he came to Glastonbury to establish the first Christian settlement in the British Isles. Thus it was that the Celts embraced the Christian faith long before it became the official religion of Rome.

The survival of Druidic culture came under severe threat following a defeat by the Romans at Anglesey in 61 CE, when by crushing the Druids they elimi-

nated one of the main sources of dissent and opposition to their rule. Much of the Celtic culture was therefore suppressed and lost, though the art and the intrinsic skill in crafts and design survived through the upheaval. With the arrival of the Christian faith, this artistic heritage found its expression in producing handwritten and illuminated Christian books, and other religious objects such as the carved high crosses and the metal shrines for holding relics of the saints. Fortunately many of the Celtic myths were preserved in manuscript form as well.

After the withdrawal of the Roman legions in 410 CE, Britain was left to defend itself from further invasion. Because of the small number of written records surviving from this period, the next 600 years are often called the Dark Ages, although this is a misnomer in other ways. It was a period when Celtic Christianity flourished through the efforts and piety of many dedicated holy men and women living in faith and simplicity, so it is also called the Golden Age of the Saints. However, it was a time of unrest and brutality too, when the Saxons, Angles and Jutes, and then the Vikings, raided and invaded the country in successive waves.

Ireland has a different story to tell. It was never conquered by the Romans and much of the Celtic culture was preserved there for a longer period than in Britain. Neither was it invaded by the Saxons, and in fact at the same time as they were overrunning parts of Britain, the Irish themselves were pushing into large areas of Wales and western Scotland. It was not until the beginning of the ninth century CE that the Vikings started to raid Ireland and to plunder the monasteries which had been founded several hundred years earlier. By this time Celtic art and design had been put to the service of the Christian faith, especially in the monasteries, to produce wonderful copies of parts of the Bible, such as *The Book of Durrow* and *The Book of Kells*.

Another noted volume was *The Gospel of Martin*, which was brought by St Ninian to Whithorn after his visit to St Martin at Tours. This book was subsequently taken to the monastic library at Movilla in Ireland, where it became the focus of a controversy between St Finian and St Columba, the latter making a secret copy of it without Finian's permission. So highly prized was the original that the terrible battle of Cuildrevne ensued in which many thousands of men died.

As a result of the deep remorse he felt for causing this battle, Columba went into self-imposed exile, eventually landing on the island of Iona, one of the Western Isles of Scotland, where he established his monastery. From Iona the light of the gospel was carried forth by many missionary monks, one of whom, St Aidan, set up another beacon of light for the Christian faith on the island of Lindisfarne, which lies off the coast of Northumbria, where the Saxon ruler had already been converted to the Christian faith.

On Aidan's arrival, the king [Oswald] appointed the island of
Lindisfarne to be his see as he asked. As the tide ebbs and flows,

*Opposite:*
Statue of St Aidan holding a torch, and the ruins of Lindisfarne Priory showing the Rainbow Arch, with a border design from *The Lindisfarne Gospels*.

this place is surrounded by sea twice a day like an island, and twice a day the sand dries and joins it to the mainland. The king always listened humbly and readily to Aidan's advice, and diligently set himself to establish and extend the Church of Christ throughout his kingdom . . .

from A *History of the English Church and People* by the Venerable Bede

Lindisfarne, or Holy Island, becomes an island only twice a day when the tide is in, as Bede explains above. At other times it is joined to the coast of Northumberland by a long metalled causeway. Stretching across the firm, ridged sand to one side of this is a succession of tall wooden poles which mark the pilgrims' route still walked by many people today, often barefoot.

On reaching the island, the ruins of the Norman abbey of St Peter, with its distinctive "rainbow arch", can be seen next to the present-day parish church. Nothing of the original Celtic buildings, which were made of wood, now remains, but there are some splendid carved stones and crosses dating from the seventh to the ninth centuries, as well as many other artefacts on display in the excellent museum nearby. In the sanctuary, at the east end of the parish church, is a handmade carpet based on a design taken from the beginning of the Gospel of St Mark in *The Lindisfarne Gospels*. The vestments used for the regular eucharistic services in the church also draw their inspiration from Celtic sources and are very finely worked in glowing colours. In the burial-ground surrounding the parish church is a striking modern sculpture of St Aidan holding a blazing torch, showing that he is still remembered as one who brought light to this place.

In addition to being a focus for worship and a base for missionary activity, some monasteries set up a scriptorium for the production of spiritual books. Here the monks copied and illustrated the texts with brightly coloured and intricate designs. *The Lindisfarne Gospels*, which date from about 700 CE, are thought to have been produced on Holy Island and are now on display in the British Museum.

In *The Lindisfarne Gospels* the first page of each of the four Gospels depicts the author, Matthew, Mark, Luke or John, in the process of writing a book or scroll. The first three evangelists are actually putting pen to paper, while John appears to have finished his writing as there is no pen in sight. Each folio also shows within the frame a creature which is used as a symbol of that evangelist. Interestingly the four symbols correspond with the four fixed signs of the zodiac which the sun is in during the four Celtic fire festivals mentioned in the previous chapter, and which hold the heavenly circle together.

Matthew, the man or angel figure, coincides with the sign of Aquarius, the water-carrier, which spans the feast of Imbolc, 1 February. Luke, the ox, occurs in the sign of Taurus, the bull, during which the feast of Beltane, 1 May, takes place. Mark, the lion, is very obviously the sign of Leo and has the feast of Lughnasad, 1 August. Finally John, whose symbol is an eagle, corresponds with

Symbols of the Evangelists from *The Lindisfarne Gospels*: St Matthew the man, St Luke the ox, St John the eagle, and St Mark the lion.

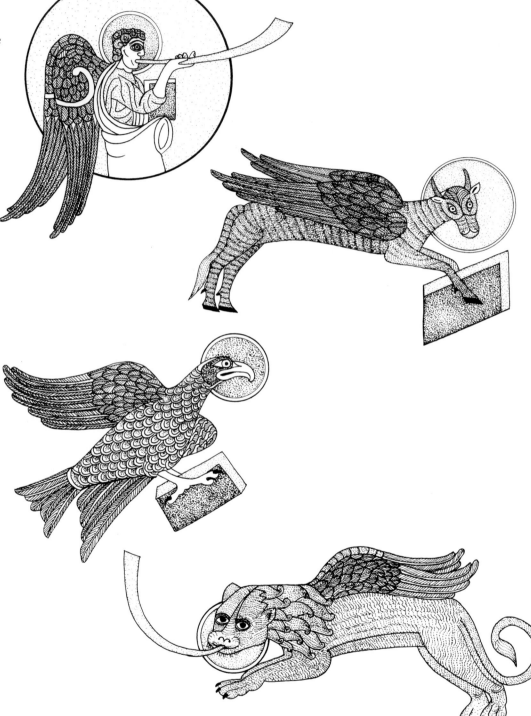

Scorpio, which in older zodiacs was shown as an eagle instead of a scorpion, and contains the feast of Samhain, 1 November.

The artist took these symbols from the final book of the Bible, the Revelation of St John, and they are part of his vision of heaven:

> In the centre, around the throne, were four living creatures, and they were covered with eyes, in front and behind. The first living creature was like a lion, the second was like an ox, the third had a face like a man, the fourth was like a flying eagle.

> Book of Revelation (ch. 4, vv. 6, 7)

Lindisfarne, its Gospels and its saintly community were like a lantern to the Celts and Saxons in Northumbria, for whom life was often brutal and short. According to the Venerable Bede, writing in the eighth century CE, St Aidan was a man of outstanding gentleness, holiness and moderation, and he won the hearts of the people by his example of kindness and generosity. St Cuthbert, who was a prior of Lindisfarne and spent most of his life in this area, was also held in great affection by the people, and his life of prayer and teaching brought the light of the Gospels to the Dark Ages.

At low tide it is possible to cross to Hobthrush Island, also called St Cuthbert's Island, where he lived before moving to the even more isolated Farne Islands. A large wooden cross marks the site of the altar within the ruins of a medieval chapel, and even more fragmentary stones in the vicinity may be the remains of his original cell.

The missionary activities of the monks from Lindisfarne penetrated deep into Saxon territory in England. One such pioneer was St Cedd, who took the Christian message to the Saxons in what is now East Anglia. He established a Christian community at Othona, a former Roman fort on the Essex coast, which is near present-day Bradwell-on-Sea. Unlike Lindisfarne, Othona is not an island but is situated in the remote marshes and mudflats of the east coast and is most easily accessible by boat. Ironically, the Roman fort was originally built to protect Britain from the Saxon invaders. Here Cedd built a chapel in 654 CE using stones from the Roman fort and dedicated it to St Peter, like Lindisfarne Priory. His shrine, along with that of his brother St Chad, is in the crypt of the church of St Mary at Lastingham in Yorkshire, and it is still a place of pilgrimage for many today.

Celtic Christians were sometimes criticized for not spreading their faith to the Saxons, but this was not true of Cedd. Coming from Lindisfarne, he belonged to the Celtic Christian tradition, but he saw the need to bring the light of the word to the pagan Saxons. When he died, thirty monks walked from Lindisfarne to Othona and lived there until all had died, except for one boy, as a mark of the great respect in which Cedd was held. The chapel is still there today and the name Othona has been adopted by a Christian community which was started just two fields away after the Second World War.

St Cuthbert's Chapel,
the Farne Islands.

The vision of this community continues in the spirit of the Celtic Church by offering hospitality to and deep care and concern for those who come to stay. They express their commitment to balance and wholeness not just in their personal lifestyle and relationships but also in taking responsibility for the wider environment. They meet for regular, prayerful worship and have permission to use the original seventh-century chapel for this purpose.

Marygate House on Holy Island is another living and thriving community which follows in the Celtic tradition. Accommodation is offered for organized groups and for individuals who wish to spend time in peace and prayer, with the choice of joining in regular corporate worship. The Reverend David Adam, the vicar of the parish, has written many authentic and moving contemporary Celtic prayers and spiritual books.

The darkness and quietness of this month of December allow us time to

focus and reflect. This slight pause in the breath of the seasonal cycle gives us an opportunity to nurture our intent to grow towards the light. It gives a moment of stillness when we can dwell with hope on the tiny seeds hidden in the earth which will come to fruition over the coming months. It encourages us to face the dark places in our own lives, which can be illumined by the light of the Gospel and by the coming Christ-light, by the words on the pages of the Scriptures and the Word made flesh in Christ Jesus. Without this necessary darkness how would we fully appreciate the light? No one sees the light like those who have known the darkness.

Christian Celts looked upon St John rather than St Peter or St Paul as their spiritual forebear and felt that their tradition of faith had come down from him. They had a special affection for the Gospel of St John, which is quite different from the other three Gospel books in that rather than being narrative it is more esoteric and portrays Christ as the Light of the World, the Creator and Sustainer of the whole universe. It speaks to the Celtic belief in the wholeness and interdependence of created order and the way in which all is redeemed and made perfect by the created Word, which is Christ.

> In the beginning was the Word, and the Word was with God, and the
> Word was God. He was with God in the beginning. Through him all
> things were made; without him nothing was made that has been
> made. In him was life, and that life was the light of men. The light
> shines in the darkness, but the darkness has not understood it.

Gospel of St John (ch. 1, vv. 1–5)

The Light and the Word are indivisibly joined. The creative word expressed in Christ is the light shining from the heart of God. He is the light that shines in the darkness of the world and also in our hearts if we ask for it to be so.

> *Thou King of the moon,*
> *Thou King of the sun,*
> *Thou King of the planets,*
> *Thou King of the stars,*
> *Thou King of the globe,*
> *Thou King of the sky,*
> *Oh! lovely Thy countenance,*
> *Thou beauteous Beam.*

from the *Carmina Gadelica* (i, 29)

# J·A·N·U·A·R·Y

*May the Son of God be at the outset of my journey,*
*May the Son of God be in surety to aid me;*
*May the Son of God make clear my way,*
*May the Son of God be at the end of my seeking.*

from the *Carmina Gadelica* (iii, 251)

WE HAVE PASSED from the old to the new through the gateway of Samhain. We have sought protection and poverty of spirit. We have asked for the light of Christ to come into our hearts. Now we consider the journey.

The Celts were inveterate travellers. They sailed great distances along the sea routes of the western coasts of Britain and Ireland and beyond, in search of trade and new lands in which to settle. They had a restlessness and a curiosity which prompted them to explore, and for the Christian monks there was a deep desire to share and spread their faith. Frequent journeys were made between the six Celtic nations, known today as Ireland, Scotland, Wales, the Isle of Man, Cornwall and Brittany. It was often easier for them to travel by sea in the typical Celtic boat, the curragh, than to undertake difficult and dangerous overland journeys. The sea was their main means of communication and these routes were of prime importance to their economic and cultural survival.

Sometimes a combination of travel by sea and land was the safest and easiest way to accomplish a journey, and to avoid rounding such hazardous headlands as Land's End a short-cut across country from coast to coast was preferable. Two examples of routes of this sort that have been reopened recently in Cornwall are the Forth an Syns, or Saints' Way, and St Michael's Way. The first runs from Padstow to Fowey and would have been used by travellers going from Wales or Ireland to Brittany. Further south, St Michael's Way spans the Penwith peninsula from Lelant near St Ives on the north coast to Marazion, the town just opposite St Michael's Mount, on the south coast. These ancient pilgrim routes have been revived with great enthusiasm and vision for leisure and devotional purposes.

Within the Celtic tradition there is a long history of tales about quests or wonder voyages called *immrama*, such as *The Voyage of Bran*, and this idea was used by the Christian Celts to explain the journey of the soul. In effect the outward journey becomes a mirror of the inner experience.

Perhaps the most famous of these early sailors was St Brendan the Voyager or Navigator. The account of his travels was one of the most fascinating and popular stories told throughout Europe in the Middle Ages, and there are many versions of the *Navigatio Brendani*. Brendan was born about 486 CE near Tralee in County Kerry, on the west coast of Ireland, and his local bishop, Erc, soon recognized his potential and sent him to a school at a monastery run by St Ita. He went on to complete his monastic training at Clonard in County Meath, where he became friends with both St Columba and St Kenneth.

Subsequently he established other monasteries in Ireland and his responsibilities grew to such an extent that he had the spiritual care of some 3,000 monks. It was at one of these monasteries, at Clonfert in County Galway, that he heard about the Delightful Island from a fellow monk called Barrind, whose disciple, Mernoc, had already settled there to lead a solitary life of prayer. Barrind had visited him and the two of them had decided to sail to the Promised Land of the Saints, which Mernoc had been to previously. Barrind and Mernoc sailed away to the west and after passing through a thick fog arrived at their destination. They walked around the island for fifteen days and eventually reached a river which flowed through the middle of it. Here they met a man who told them to cease their explorations as they had seen enough of this heavenly place where there was no need of food, drink or clothing, and where night never fell and the day never ended. The two monks returned to the Delightful Island, their clothes bearing the fragrance of Paradise, and told some other monks who had come to join Mernoc about their journey.

When he heard this story, Brendan decided that he wanted to visit the Promised Land of the Saints for himself. To this end he went to the west coast of Ireland with fourteen monks and there they built a boat using traditional methods and materials: a wooden frame covered with ox-hides tanned with oak bark and the seams greased on the outside with fat. When they had loaded spare materials and food, and fitted a mast, sail and steering equipment, they

*Opposite:*
St Brendan.

went on board the boat, blessing it in the name of the Father, Son and Holy Spirit. In customary manner, they had fasted for forty days before setting sail. Tradition tells that Brendan made plans for his epic voyage on Hungry Hill, high above the sweep of Bantry Bay in County Cork.

St Brendan and the brothers had many adventures at sea. On one occasion the boat ran aground on a whale which the monks thought was an island. They had even started cooking a meal when the island began to move. Being terrified by this experience, they hastily climbed back into their boat and sailed away. Brendan had been warned by God in a dream that the island was in reality a whale and so he was able to calm and comfort his companions.

*Be Thou a smooth way before me,*
*Be Thou a guiding star above me,*
*Be Thou a keen eye behind me,*
*This day, this night, for ever.*

*If only Thou, O God of life,*
*Be at peace with me, be my support,*
*Be to me as a star, be to me as a helm,*
*From my lying down in peace to my rising anew.*

from the *Carmina Gadelica* (iii, 171)

Another time they encountered a huge pillar of bright crystal, an iceberg, reaching up to the sky. They came close to it and as it floated through the sea they examined its base and sailed along its sides for four days. On the iceberg Brendan found a chalice and a paten, and praised the Lord Jesus for providing these two vessels to hold the bread and the wine for Holy Communion.

He and his companions visited one particular island during a volcanic eruption which sounded like a blacksmith's forge, with the blowing of bellows and the tremor of iron hammers on an anvil. It seemed as if the inhabitants of the island were showering them with burning missiles. The sailors prayed to Jesus Christ for deliverance from the place and its molten lava, which was being spewed into the sea. They finally escaped by raising the sail even higher and rowing away as fast as they could.

On their journeyings the monastic band visited other islands. One was small and round with no soil and only bare rock. They approached the cliffs with difficulty and on landing met Paul the Hermit, who had lived there for ninety years. He had no clothes and was covered only with his beard and body hair. The first fifty years of his life had been spent at the monastery of St Patrick, who on the day after his death had appeared to Paul in a vision and instructed him to get into a boat which would take him to the place where he was to spend the rest of his life. For the first thirty years on the remote island Paul had been fed by an otter which brought him a fish every three days, and for the last sixty years he had been nourished by water from a small spring. Paul told Brendan and the monks about the next stage of their journey in search of the Promised Land of the Saints and, after he had blessed them, they sailed away.

Most of the islands which Brendan visited were already inhabited and on several occasions he went to the Island of the Community of Ailbe, which had a company of twenty-four monks that had been established eighty years earlier. On another island, which had a huge number of sheep, there was a man who told Brendan and his companions about the next stage of their quest.

There was yet another island which was very flat and without trees but had plenty of large fruit. Here Brendan left one of his party who wished to join the three choirs which lived there singing and praising God daily.

After many years and numerous voyages Brendan and his companions did eventually reach the Promised Land of the Saints. They had with them as a guide the man from the Island of Sheep, and after sailing for forty days and passing through the thick fog they came ashore on the island which Barrind had described. They explored it and found the river flowing through the middle. Here a man met them and told them they had reached the end of their quest. He also instructed Brendan to gather the fruit of the land and collect the precious stones from the ground before sailing back to his home country, where he would soon die. Brendan returned home, first to the Delightful Island and then to his fellow monks in Ireland, and told them of all his adventures and how God had richly blessed him. Soon afterwards he did indeed die.

Protect me, O Lord, for my boat is so small.
Protect me, O Lord, for my boat is so small.
My boat is so small and your sea is so wide.
Protect me, O Lord.

Breton fishermen's prayer

In all the excitement and adventure it is easy to overlook the fact that these voyages are woven around a Christian calendar, with Lent, Easter and Pentecost as the focal points, and also around a monastic discipline of worship and prayer at regular times during the day. It is as if the writer is affirming that all human journeys, with their endeavour and discovery, must be seen in an eternal context and rhythm. Journeys make sense when taken within a sacred framework of times and seasons, even if we come to realize this only in retrospect. *The Voyage of Brendan* is an old story but we can, with a little imagination, identify with his experiences on the various islands and find parallels to incidents and situations in our own lives.

There are many places associated with St Brendan. On the Dingle peninsula in Ireland there is a village called Brandon, where the neighbouring bay, headland and mountain all bear the same name, a form of the word

Entrance to the
Gallarus Oratory,
County Kerry.

Brendan. The Gallarus Oratory, a dry-stone construction shaped like an upturned boat with sloping, corbelled walls and roof, is situated here on the peninsula too. Built on a rectangular ground plan approximately 15 feet long and 10 feet wide, it may date from as early as the eighth century CE. It is sited about 250 yards away from the Saints' Road, the main pilgrim route to Mount Brandon, and it has been suggested that this was because the mountain was visible from the oratory but not from the track. This style of building was also used for the beehive cells found on Skellig Michael and other places on the west coast of Ireland.

Some of the places visited by the sailor-saint on his travels can be readily identified, as Tim Severin has shown in his account, *The Brendan Voyage*. He and other scholars have cited the Hebrides, St Kilda, Rockall, the Faroe Islands, Iceland, Jan Mayen Island, Greenland and Newfoundland as possible places which the saint visited. In the Faroe Islands there is Brandarsvik, meaning Brendan's Creek. Other islands further south in the Atlantic have been

identified with the Bahamas and Jamaica in the West Indies and Madeira off the coast of Africa.

Despite the emphasis so far on the sea, the Celtic saints did travel by land as well. St Brendan's forays were matched by the overland journeys of St Columbanus and St Gall in Europe. There were many of these wandering monks, who were known as *peregrini*, and they spread the Christian faith wherever they went. Monastic settlements were established by Columbanus at Luxeuil in France and at Bobbio in northern Italy. According to Swiss legend, Columbanus stayed by Lake Zurich, where there are two lakeside villages known as Iona and Staffa, places that would have been familiar to him or his fellow missionary monks in their homeland.

St Gall's plan for the monastery which he established in Switzerland became the accepted blueprint for monastic settlements throughout the whole of Europe, and his name is still preserved in the title of the canton of St Gallen. It is paradoxical that the Celtic *peregrini* carried their faith across Europe in the sixth and seventh centuries CE almost to the holy city of Rome.

The long journeys of the *peregrini* were inspired by the Christian belief that here on earth we have "no abiding city". Their example was our distant spiritual ancestor Abraham, who was told by God to leave his country, his people and his father's household, and go to the land which God would show him. Thus he became the founder of the Jewish people, who referred to him as "a wandering Aramaean".

Sometimes these itinerant monks lost sight of their spiritual calling and brought disrepute upon themselves. At the beginning of his monastic rule, written early in the sixth century CE, St Benedict mentions four kinds of monks: those who live in a monastery serving under a rule and an abbot; those who after the training and discipline of life in a monastery then live as solitary hermits; those who live in groups of two or three but without any training or discipline; and finally those who "spend their whole lives wandering from province to province staying three days in one monastery and four in another, ever roaming and never stable, given up to their own wills and the allurements of gluttony". The third and fourth groups are condemned by St Benedict, and particularly the last.

Fortunately to redress the balance we have the good example of leaders like St Columbanus and St Gall, who, even though they covered great distances, never lost sight of the monastic roots which had nurtured them, and founded many new Christian settlements in the course of their travels.

> I am weary, weak and cold,
> I am weary of travelling land and sea,
> I am weary of traversing moorland and billow,
> Grant me peace in the nearness of Thy repose
> This night.

from the *Carmina Gadelica* (iii, 177)

Another journey which we might remember this month is that of the Magi, or Wise Men from the East, who visited Jesus in Bethlehem, bringing their familiar gifts of gold, incense and myrrh. This is commemorated at Epiphany, or the Feast of the Star, on 6 January and celebrates the showing forth of Christ to the world. In Ireland on this evening it was customary to light twelve candles and arrange them in a circle, and then place a larger thirteenth candle in the centre "in memory of the Saviour and his Apostles, lights of the world".

There are some organized pilgrimages held in Britain and Ireland during the year which anyone can join: for instance, at Glastonbury, Holywell in north Wales, Haddington in Scotland and Croagh Patrick in Ireland. If you prefer to journey alone, there are pilgrim routes that can be followed to various sacred places, such as St Davids in Wales. At Glencolumbkille, County Donegal, in north-west Ireland there is a recognized short pilgrimage known as *an Turas* meaning The Journey. Here the pilgrim does a 3-mile walk, usually barefoot, using specific set prayers and devotions at each stopping point or station, including St Colmcille's Well. This rite is most often performed at the feast of St Colmcille, also known as St Columba, on 9 June, but can be done at any time of the year.

In reality it is not always possible for us to go on a pilgrimage journey because of family responsibilities, work commitments, lack of funds, illness or other reasons, but through the ages ways have been found to encourage the pilgrim to go forward despite these possible external difficulties. The maze or labyrinth is one such answer. In a Christian context it represents the journey to knowledge and salvation, or even to the Heavenly City. These designs can often be found in churches and cathedrals, especially on the continent of Europe.

There are some labyrinth patterns carved on stone that have interesting Celtic connections, like the one found at Hollywood in County Wicklow and now in the National Museum of Ireland in Dublin, and the two carvings in Rocky Valley near Tintagel in Cornwall. The Irish stone was discovered close to an ancient pilgrim route to Glendalough known as St Kevin's Road. The two mazes in Cornwall are located towards the seaward end of a lovely valley known as St Nectan's Glen, where the sixth-century hermit is said to have lived.

These examples are all seven-circuit labyrinths with a cross at the centre. This means that from the entry point one makes seven sweeping, almost circular, movements around and back across the maze to reach the middle. It is like an elegant dance, and many large mazes were constructed to be used for ceremonial purposes. Once in the centre, it is necessary to turn and retrace your steps, again circling seven times to the exit.

One of the most prominent ancient mazes extant today is that encircling the Tor at Glastonbury. It is thought to be a ritual pathway, although it has only recently been acknowledged as such.

This threading of the maze is like a pilgrimage. It provides a structure within which we can explore things outside the ordinary; it is a world apart. A labyrinth can be "walked" with the eyes, as a meditation. It isn't necessary to

*Below*:
The Hollywood Stone
from County Wicklow,
now in the National
Museum of Ireland in
Dublin.

leave your home, or even your armchair, to go on this spiritual journey. All pilgrims need stopping places for recollection and recreation, and the changes in direction at the turning points in the maze are the equivalent of these pauses. It expresses the path of life in a linear form, like a single continuous thread. Textile techniques like knitting or knotting which, unlike weaving, use just one long thread are known as "tangle-thread" mazes, and such running designs were used as protective charms on the thresholds of houses in Scotland, and incidentally also in India.

Maze carved on a
Norman font in
Lewannick Church,
Cornwall.

The word labyrinth comes from the Greek *labrys*, meaning double-axe. This double-axe shape resembles one of the pagan symbols for the Goddess, the butterfly – a concept which expresses so well the idea of transformation and rebirth, relating in turn to the purpose of the maze. It is the journey not the destination which matters here.

*May God be with thee in every pass,*
*Jesus be with thee on every knoll,*
*Spirit be with thee by water's roll,*
    *On headland, on ridge, and on grass;*

*Each sea and land, each moor and each mead,*
*Each eve's lying-down, each rising's morn,*
*In the wave-trough, or on foam-crest borne,*
    *Each step which thy journey doth lead.*

from *Poems of the Western Highlanders*

# F·E·B·R·U·A·R·Y

On Saint Bride's Day the nests start to grow,
The building ravens fly to and fro,
And wheeling rooks activity show;
O feast of Saint Bride, feast of the maid,
White-fingered Bride of the music played.

from *Poems of the Western Highlanders*

*T*HE CELTIC FEAST of Imbolc, or Oimelc, is at the beginning of the Roman month of February and is the second fire festival of the Celtic year. The name means "ewe's milk" and it is the time of spring sowing and when lambs are born, bringing with them the promise of warmer, lighter days.

I *will go out to sow the seed,*
In *name of Him who gave it growth;*
I *will place my front in the wind,*
And *throw a gracious handful on high.*

from the *Carmina Gadelica* (i, 243)

The feast day of St Bridget of Kildare falls on 1 February, and also at this time of Imbolc comes the Christian festival of Candlemas on 2 February, when the Church celebrates the Purification of the Virgin Mary and the Presentation of Christ in the Temple at Jerusalem. In Scotland it is said that St Bridget, or St Bride, walked in front of Mary with a lighted candle in each hand as she went to the Temple, and even though the wind was strong and the flames unprotected they did not flicker or go out.

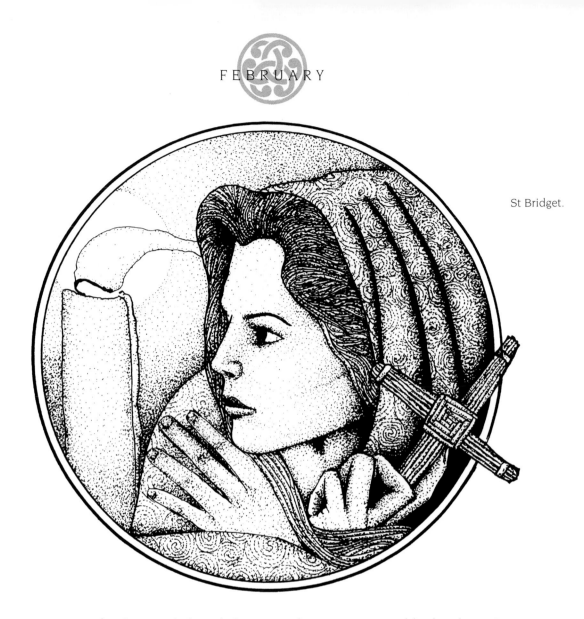

St Bridget.

In Ireland it was believed that St Bridget, accompanied by her favourite white cow, went around the countryside on the eve of her feast, on 31 January, imparting her blessing to homes and livestock alike.

*The charm put by Bride the beneficent,*
*On her goats, on her sheep, on her kine,*
*On her horses, on her chargers, on her herds,*
*Early and late going home, and from home.*

from the *Carmina Gadelica* (ii, 35)

In some places offerings such as cake and bread were placed outside to welcome her presence, and often a sheaf of corn was added for her cow. This food was expected to be taken away by passing tramps or poor people.

A better-known custom is that of making a St Bridget's Cross, known in Irish as *cros Bríde* or *bogha Bríde*. The entire process was a ritual, and when completed the cross was sprinkled with holy water and hung above the door

with a prayer of blessing, where it remained as a protection and sign of plenty for the whole year. The most common type resembles the "God's Eye" design found in South America and is a diamond or lozenge made of straw wound on a wooden cross-shape frame. Another type, made of rushes, has a square centre with three or four projecting arms. It was customary to have a celebratory meal and a cake called *bairín-breac* was baked for the occasion. Fresh butter was always churned on this day and formed part of the fare.

At the summit of Glastonbury Tor, on the tower which is all that remains of St Michael's Church, there is a carving of Bride with her cow, a reminder of the tradition that she once visited this place. However, she is more usually associated with Kildare in Ireland, where she founded first a nunnery and then a double monastery for monks and nuns. Kildare means "church of the oak", which reveals the pagan origins of the place. It is more famous today for its racecourse, the Curragh, than for any links with St Bridget. Nothing remains of her original foundation, but the Church of Ireland cathedral which stands on an ancient site is dedicated to her and there is also a holy well at nearby Tully which bears her name.

In Uist in the Western Isles, the flocks were counted on 1 February and dedicated to St Bride. The people had songs and blessings for each agricultural task: there were prayers for herding and driving cattle, for shearing and for churning butter. Milking croons were intoned to soothe the cattle and to encourage them to give their milk. Some beasts became so used to this treatment that they would withhold their milk until their favourite lilt was sung.

> Bless, O God, my little cow,
> >  Bless, O God, my desire;
> Bless Thou my partnership
> >  And the milking of my hands, O God.
>
> from the *Carmina Gadelica* (iv, 65)

There were even prayers and blessings for the seaweed which the people relied upon as a fertilizer for their crops.

In Brittany there are processions each year in honour of the numerous Celtic saints who are patrons of the different farm animals such as cattle, pigs, horses and sheep. Prayers are said and the animals blessed. Nowadays it is mainly horses which are brought, but it has been known for tractors to be blessed as well, showing how the tradition is adapting to new circumstances. Many Breton churches have statues of these early Celtic Christians with their particular animals.

By the very nature of their pastoral lifestyle, the Celts lived according to the turning of the seasons and depended upon close relationships with their domesticated animals. These provided not only food but also other benefits which made life richer and easier: horses were a speedy means of transport and communication, and in warfare horse-drawn chariots ensured Celtic

dominance; sheep were an abundant source of wool for clothing; and dogs were used for hunting and protection. Hunters would ask permission before taking the life of a creature for food; animals were treated with great respect and had their own rightful places in the Celts' sacred view of life.

Reflecting this attitude, animals are frequently found as motifs in Celtic art. Although at first they may appear to be mere decoration, they were often used as a form of hieroglyph to convey an idea or a value. This concept is also apparent in the ancient Druidic teachings, in which animals were especially revered, both for their individual qualities and deeper allegorical meanings, and for their ability to journey between the worlds, as guardians and guides.

We are all familiar with the bull as a symbol of strength and the dove as a sign of peace and purity, but the Celtic pantheon was much broader. To give some examples, a salmon represented wisdom, a boar was a symbol of the warrior spirit, a goose was an image of vigilance and a hare meant rebirth. These correlations sometimes prove to be unerringly accurate: for instance, geese are used as guards in the environs of some Scottish whisky distilleries in the present day, as they can be very fierce and threatening, and of course very vocal with their warning calls if approached. The Christian Iona Community uses the wild goose, rather than the more familiar dove, as their symbol of the Holy Spirit because of its wildness.

Each monastic foundation required copies of the scriptures and prayer books to satisfy the ecclesiastical and liturgical needs of the community and the use of animal ornament came to its zenith in some of the highly decorated manuscripts produced by Celtic Christian scribes. The crowning glory of their art is surely *The Book of Kells*, now housed in Trinity College, Dublin. The variety and complexity of the ornamentation and design in this particular manuscript make it an unparalleled example, not only of the superb techniques of these early artists but also as a means of conveying the Christian message. It is rich with Eucharistic symbolism in which animals, mainly native species, figure widely as interlinear ornament. We find a cat pursuing a rat which is holding a Communion wafer, a hound chasing a hare, an otter catching a fish; there are also a cockerel and his hens, a she-goat and a deer.

The monks took ideas from both the wild and the domestic animals they were familiar with and saw around them. *The Lindisfarne Gospels*, written and illuminated on sea-girt Holy Island, contain many representations of sea-birds, some of which are recognizable as particular species.

In *The Book of Kells* the face of Christ is displayed often throughout the text and he is shown as a blond young man, not a dark-haired Jew. The Celtic royalty had fair hair and so favour was shown towards the golden-haired. Again, animal symbols usually accompany the Saviour, most commonly a salmon, but also a snake, a lion and a peacock. Here we have four beasts from each of the four elements, water, earth, fire and air respectively, and this demonstrates his authority and rule over all creation. The fish was used by the first Christians as a symbol for Christ, as the initial letters of the Greek word for fish, *ichthus*, form

Animals from
*The Book of Kells.*

an acronym and stand for "Jesus Christ, Son of God, Saviour". This condenses an important message, but also introduces the idea that Jesus ushered in the Age of Pisces, which is the constellation of the Jewish nation.

The elongated interlace patterns are sometimes made up of the second creature, the snake or serpent, which meanders right around the border of some pages. It was chosen because of its ability to shed its skin and start a new life. Thus this reptile has come to symbolize the Resurrection of Christ from the dead. However, in the book of Genesis the snake was taken to represent the principle of evil, so it could have more than one meaning.

The lion was also used to symbolize the Resurrection. There was an Eastern tradition, known in Ireland, that lion-cubs were born dead and were brought to life only three days later by their father breathing on them or roaring. This story is reminiscent of the three-day interval between the Crucifixion on Good Friday and the rising of Christ to new life on Easter Day. Peacocks are used to show the immortality and incorruptibility of Christ, drawn from an ancient belief that the flesh of this bird did not putrefy.

Fine examples of powerful animal forms can also be seen on early metalwork treasures such as the silver-gilt Gundestrup Cauldron, which was found ritually laid out in pieces on the surface of a Danish peat bog in 1891. It is thought to have been made about 100 BCE and shows the pre-Christian god Cernunnos with his antlers. Recently it has been suggested that the figure may depict a Celtic shaman working in the form of a stag. Shape-shifting and the ability to move between the worlds with shifts of consciousness were a source of power for the Druids, and the resulting spiritual vision was much respected by the Celtic peoples. It is said that some of the saints, like Columba and Patrick, also possessed such expertise and were capable of transformation.

From this belief comes the story of how St Patrick and a band of his followers changed themselves into the form of deer to escape attack from King Laoghaire's troops. This is when the great invocation called "The Deer's Cry", perhaps more familiarly known to us as "St Patrick's Breastplate", is said to

Designs from the Gundestrup Cauldron, Copenhagen.

have been written, although it probably dates from the eighth century CE. Here the saint calls on all the elements of creation to aid him:

*I arise today*
*Through the strength of heaven:*
*Light of sun,*
*Radiance of moon,*
*Splendour of fire,*
*Speed of lightning,*
*Swiftness of wind,*
*Depth of sea,*
*Stability of earth,*
*Firmness of rock.*

translated from the Irish by Kuno Meyer

One of the earliest places of pilgrimage in Ireland was Glendalough, in the mountains of County Wicklow. Pilgrims came from all over Ireland to see and touch the tomb of St Kevin, who lived in the valley and died in 618 CE. Because he wanted to become a hermit, he was attracted by the remoteness of the location, and so founded his monastery here. The continuing importance of the site is shown by the presence of an ancient paved road that was constructed through the gap in the Wicklow Mountains for pilgrims coming from the west.

Glendalough attracts many thousands of visitors and pilgrims each year with its glorious scenery and the diversity of its historic remains. The whole complex of buildings is dominated by a round tower, over 100 feet high, which may have served various purposes as a watch-tower, storehouse and place of refuge. For the pilgrim it was a landmark which showed that the journey was nearly complete. Glendalough has been called a "monastic city" because of the numerous ecclesiastical buildings and sites in the valley. In addition to the round tower, there are several churches, a ruined cathedral, a gateway, a priests' house and a circular stone-walled enclosure known as the Caher, where pilgrims could shelter after completing their journey. St Kevin's name is preserved in a church called St Kevin's House, a stone clochan called St Kevin's Cell, and a cave above the Upper Lake, where he used to retire for prayer and to sleep, called St Kevin's Bed.

Living closely with nature, often in secluded places, the Celtic saints were so in harmony with creation that the birds and the beasts became their regular and devoted companions, and indeed some of the most charming stories about this affinity involve St Kevin. On one occasion while he was praying a blackbird came and nested in his hand and, rather than disturb it, St Kevin remained in position until the eggs were hatched. Another time an otter retrieved St Kevin's psalter, which he had dropped into the lake, and a further story relates how a wild boar took refuge in his cell from huntsmen and their dogs.

It is said that the first disciples of the sixth-century Cornish abbot St Piran

were a fox, a badger, a boar, a calf and a doe. Delightful though the idea is of him preaching and ministering to these creatures, it is possible that each of them was the totem animal of a particular tribe and as such represented a body of people. Through meditation each of us can discover our own totem animal or animals, and learn from their behaviour and characteristics. They can often represent the unexplored parts of our psyche. If this appeals, they can become our companions, teachers and guides on our spiritual journey.

Memories of the saints linger on in the folk-names of various creatures. In Ireland the linnet is known as "Bridget's bird" and the oystercatcher as "Bridget's page". The black and white eider ducks, common around the coast of Northumberland, are often called "Cuddy's ducks" or "Cuthbert's ducks", recalling how the saint loved them the best of all God's creatures.

In our arrogance we might assume that man is superior, but sensitivity and communication do not always flow just from man to animal; this is a two-way process. An old white horse that was used by the monks on Iona to carry milk pails from the byre to the monastery instinctively knew when St Columba was going to die. The saint, although frail, made his way to a nearby barn to bless two large mounds of winnowed corn which would be used by the community to make their bread throughout the coming year. On his return journey, although the distance was not great, he sat down to rest. The white horse approached and, leaning his great head against Columba's chest, wept tears of sorrow, knowing that the saint was soon to leave this world. The saint's companion wanted to chase the animal away but Columba forbade him. Instead he blessed the beast, which duly turned away mournfully.

Another early Celtic saint, Colman of Kilmacduagh, appears to have had a very special relationship with three unlikely members of the animal kingdom: a cockerel, a mouse and a fly. The service of Lauds takes place during the hours of darkness and instead of having the usual bell to awaken him for prayer, Colman had the services of a cockerel which would crow loudly to rouse him. The monk's Rule was strict and his hours of rest very short, so that sometimes he found it difficult to stay awake, but his holy vows were so important to him that the mouse would come and pull at his clothing and even nibble at his ear to keep him attentive to his divine office. The fly aided him during his waking hours, for it would walk up and down each line of his spiritual texts as he read, and if he had to leave the book to attend to something else it would sit at the end of the line, awaiting his return, so that he would not lose his place.

It is perhaps puzzling for the modern reader to understand why the lives of these saints contain such quaint stories. We find them strange because in our urban and industrialized society, we are largely out of touch with the elements and the land, and hence our relationships with the wild creatures that inhabit the countryside and field have suffered. Instead, we value animals because of their use to us, whether as food, or for companionship or en-tertainment, and not because we and they are all part of God's created world. Conditioned by years of exploiting the environment, including animals, we

have only begun to realize relatively recently that the human race is just another species, like the cockerel, the mouse or the fly, and that we are interdependent with everything else in the global ecosystem. We could become extinct, just as some species have, if we do not learn to live in harmony with our environment and to respect other living creatures.

The Christian Celts had a completely different view of life. They acknowledged the totality of their surroundings and embraced both the natural world and their own man-made environment. They were not pantheistic and did not worship nature or animals, but they did have a deep reverence for creation, sensing the pattern and order of the cosmos and how all is infused with the divine spirit.

This was expressed very strongly not only in their art, as we have seen, but also in their artefacts. At first glance it seems that every available surface is covered with ornamentation and design, but this decoration is not merely surface detail. It speaks of a culture and a people for whom each everyday object fitted into a supreme sacred plan. By ornamenting their tools, weapons, clothing and other articles, each item was sanctified and revealed this purpose and meaning; they were a constant reminder of order in the seeming chaos.

Perhaps one of the less helpful trends of our modern society is the cult of the individual, and consequently we are often encouraged to feel separate from our neighbour. The truth is that whatever we may feel, we are all part of the divine creation and indivisibly joined to each other. It is important to remember that we do not go on pilgrimage alone, even if we are not in the company of others. Both the green movement, which has become so relevant and popular in recent decades, and the revival of interest in the Celtic and the Native American and Wiccan traditions, speak strongly of this interdependence.

The intricate knotwork patterns which can still be seen today on such monuments as the South Cross at Clonmacnois in Ireland and in the illuminated manuscripts like *The Book of Durrow* and *The Book of Kells* symbolize how each part of the creation is linked with every other part. This was understood instinctively by the Celts, and may help to explain the lure of sacred sites such as Glendalough for the modern pilgrim.

> *I wish, O Son of the living God, O ancient, eternal King,*
> *For a hidden little hut in the wilderness that it may be my dwelling.*
>
> *An all-grey lithe little lark to be by its side,*
> *A clear pool to wash away sins through the grace of the Holy Spirit.*
>
> *Quite near, a beautiful wood around it on every side,*
> *To nurse many-voiced birds, hiding it with its shelter.*
>
> *A southern aspect for warmth, a little brook across its floor,*
> *A choice land with many gracious gifts such as be good for every plant.*
>
> translated from the Irish by Kuno Meyer

# M·A·R·C·H

*On Saint Patrick's Day Bride bending low*
*Both her hands bathed in the river-flow;*
*Off the cold-bearing mother did go;*
*The Night of Saint Bride supper and light*
*But sleep and light for Saint Patrick's Night.*

from *Poems of the Western Highlanders*

*T*HE MONTH of March contains the spring or vernal equinox, when the sun has reached the half-way point on its journey north and passed from the zodiacal sign of Pisces into Aries, the ram. Day and night are of equal length, but from this moment the daylight begins to grow stronger than the darkness. It is spring and the whole of creation is coming alive in a very visible way; new life is all around. By St Patrick's Day, 17 March, the days are becoming milder too. Lady Day falls towards the end of this month on 25 March; this is the feast of the Annunciation, when Mary was told by the archangel Gabriel that she would conceive and bear a son, Jesus.

The Druids believed that the source of all life was water and that it existed in purity before the world was created. It was the first principle and remained unsullied until it became blended with the earth. In the Celtic mind, therefore, water was life-giving, and where it flowed from the body of the earth at wells and in springs it was both valued and venerated. Every small community would have had its own water sources that were regarded as having magical and healing properties, sometimes for specific illnesses, and as evidence of these beliefs many votive offerings have been found in wells, lakes and rivers.

The source of the River Boyne in Ireland is traditionally the Well of Segais, also said to be the source of all knowledge. Nine hazel trees grew around this

legendary pool and as the nuts dropped into the water they released bubbles of inspiration, or were eaten by the salmon of wisdom.

The Christian Celts would have found similarities between their own ideas about water and the stories of creation in the book of Genesis, where the earth is described as formless and empty, with darkness over the surface of the deep and the Spirit of God hovering over the water. They would also have recognized the description of creation where streams came up from the earth to water the whole surface of the ground, because the Lord God had not sent rain on the earth. Both Druidic and Christian belief affirmed the primacy of water for starting and sustaining life on earth.

As the transition from Druidism to Christianity took place, the custom of visiting these sources for healing and divination did not change; rather the emphasis shifted from the place being "magic" to being "holy", and associations with particular saints were encouraged. There are many hundreds of wells in Britain, Ireland and Brittany named after the early Celtic saints, and the majority of these would have had pagan origins. Indeed some of the water deities have been Christianized too, with the name of a saint being substituted for the original guardian of the place.

St Nectan's Glen in Cornwall is a good example of this. Nechtan was a pagan Celtic water god whose position was superseded by the Welsh St Nectan, an early hermit who settled beside the waterfall and pool here.

*It is from Nectan's mossy steep,*
  *The foamy waters flash and leap:*
*It is where shrinking wild-flowers grow,*
  *They lave the nymph that dwells below.*

from *The Sisters of Glen Nectan* by R. S. Hawker

In this verse the water-nymph is still in evidence as an inhabitant of the place despite St Nectan's presence. Perhaps surprisingly, these lines were written by an Anglican clergyman of the nineteenth century, Robert Stephen Hawker. He was born in Plymouth in 1804 and became the vicar of Morwenstow on the north coast of Cornwall, where he lived for most of his life. Within the grounds of his vicarage was the holy well of St John in the Wilderness, the water of which was used for christenings. Although he was considered eccentric by many, some of his activities were akin to those of the early Celtic saints. Certain items of his clothing displayed how he identified with their customs, and also the life of his Lord and Saviour. He wore a woollen fisherman's jersey, which not only brought him closer to his own parishioners, many of whom were fishermen, but also reminded them that Jesus was a "fisher of men". Embroidered on it was a bold red cross in the place where the spear entered Christ's body on the cross, and blood and water flowed out. He had a profound concern for shipwrecked sailors, many of whom perished on the rocks along the

St Nectan's Kieve,
Cornwall.

wild coast of his parish, and took part in a number of rescues, afterwards giving those poor, unfortunate seamen who were saved shelter, food and clothing until they were well enough to leave the area. Also he carried a walking stick with a cross-shaped handle which he called his pastoral staff, reminiscent of St Patrick's own staff, which was known as *Bachall Íosa* or "Staff of Jesus".

He had a particular devotion to St Cuthbert and possessed a stole copied from one which had been placed on the body of the saint in his shrine at Durham. Cuthbert spent long years of his life in isolation as a hermit on the island of Inner Farne. Here he prayed and meditated to the roar of the ocean and the calling of sea-birds. Hawker felt that his coastal parish had similarities

and so he constructed a hut for himself in a solitary spot high on the cliffs, looking out to sea. Hawker's Hut is now owned by the National Trust and can be visited by today's pilgrim.

The Celtic monks usually established their settlements close to a convenient water supply, for obvious reasons, and often the appearance of a spring of water was seen as a sign of divine approval of a chosen site. However, even these seemingly heaven-sent supplies could be reduced to a trickle in a hot summer and become inadequate for a community's needs. St David of Wales, whose feast day falls on the first day of this month, was reputed to have had great power over the element of water and on just such an occasion he withdrew to a nearby solitary place for prayer, and as he interceded a new spring of clear water bubbled up.

It was not only his monks who benefited from St David's ability to tap underground water supplies. A farmer named Terdi came to the saint asking for help as the river was a good distance away and he found it very tiring to carry water to his crops. David responded to the man's request and after prayer he dug in the soil with his staff; miraculously a bubbling fountain appeared which flowed continually through the hot weather.

St David was known as "the Waterman" or "David who lives on water". As March usually embraces most of the season of Lent, it is perhaps appropriate this month to remember his simplicity and abstinence. He lived a frugal and austere life, rejecting wine, fermented liquor and everything intoxicating, existing on only bread, water and vegetables, and he expected his fellow monks to do the same. However, when some special guests came to visit his monastic community, he extended his hospitality beyond this basic fare to include fish as well. His asceticism is further demonstrated by his practice of standing for long hours in cold water, reciting the psalms.

When Gerald of Wales visited the city of St David's in 1188, he described it as being in a "remote corner of the country, exposed to the winds and to extremely inclement weather, with rocky and barren soil and no rivers or pasture-lands". Surely an unpromising location for St David to settle? Although St David's may seem relatively inaccessible to us today, the site of his monastery was carefully chosen so that it was close to both the sea and a small river. The major sea routes, north–south and east–west, intersected here and brought visitors and traders from Ireland, north Wales, south-west Britain, Brittany and the Mediterranean to the St David's peninsula. They were able to enter numerous small, safe harbours such as Porth Clais, Solva, Porth Stinian and Whitesands Bay, all only a short distance from St David's. The River Alun flows through the peninsula to Porth Clais and a mile upstream from the harbour, in a marshy valley sheltered from the prevailing westerly winds and out of sight of Irish raiders, David established his monastic community.

The present low-lying cathedral stands on the site of his original church, which was burnt down in 645 CE. Behind the high altar in the Holy Trinity Chapel the bones of both St David and his confessor and soul-friend, the

The Abraham
Stone, St David's
Cathedral, Dyfed.

The Great Cross,
Nevern, Dyfed.

Breton St Stinian, lie together in a reliquary in a recess in the wall. Also in the cathedral are three marker stones of a type found on an imaginary line running from the east of Ireland to Herefordshire. Simple in design, they occur near early churches dedicated to the saint, perhaps marking pilgrim routes.

In the Middle Ages St David's attracted many pilgrims, as two visits here equalled one visit to Rome. Adjacent to the cathedral are the imposing ruins of the Bishop's Palace, where at one time many pilgrims were given hospitality. Nearby on the coast stands a fourteenth-century pilgrims' chapel dedicated to St Non, David's mother, and also a well named after her. This, together with the

Statue of the
Virgin Mary,
opposite St Non's
Well, Dyfed.

small ruined chapel next to it, traditionally marks his birthplace. The spring is said to have risen at his birth and is credited with healing powers, especially for rheumatism and eye disorders. Before the Reformation the water used to be taken to the cathedral and consecrated for use in the liturgies. The whole peninsula is rich in sites and lore associated with St David and his contemporaries, and there is much to see.

There were well-established pilgrim routes to and from St David's, one of which covered the entire length of Wales northwards to Holywell on Deeside, where the holy well dedicated to St Winefride was also a focus of devotion. Holywell claims to be the only major place of pilgrimage which escaped the destruction of relics and sacred sites during the Reformation in the sixteenth century. Today there remains a large star-shaped well within a medieval stone building which opens on to an expanse of water like a swimming-pool. Here pilgrims come to bathe and to be healed, passing through the water three times. This number is significant, as the ancient Celts baptized by triple immersion. Regular services are still held here and there are major pilgrimages organized by the Roman Catholic and Orthodox Churches each year.

For the Christian Celts, these ideas of the sacredness and healing power of water had biblical precedent. In the Old Testament, according to the Mosaic laws, water was used for ceremonial cleansing and there were strict observances surrounding its use. Also related is how Moses struck a rock twice with his staff, causing water to gush out so that his people and their livestock could drink in the desert. The strong imagery in this story of Moses and his wanderings in the desert inspired a Welsh hymn-writer to pen the famous "Guide me, O Thou Great Jehovah", with the following verse:

> Open now the crystal fountain
> Whence the healing stream doth flow;
> Let the fiery cloudy pillar
> Lead me all my journey through:
> Strong Deliverer,
> Be Thou still my strength and shield.

> W. Williams (1716–91)

For the Christian Celts the use of wells for healing followed the pattern of the story of the pool of Bethesda in the New Testament.

> Now there is in Jerusalem near the Sheep Gate a pool, which in
> Aramaic is called Bethesda and which is surrounded by five covered
> colonnades. Here a great number of disabled people used to lie –
> the blind, the lame, the paralysed.

> Gospel of St John (ch. 5, vv. 2,3)

The water was supposed to have been stirred at certain times by an angel, which released its miraculous curative powers. It is not difficult to imagine how these powerful images could be transferred to the immediate environment of the Christian believer who already had a traditional source of healing in the vicinity.

Cornwall is especially rich in holy wells, having around 200 known sites, some of which are still used for both healing and divinatory purposes. At Madron, north of Penzance, the pagan and the Christian exist side by side, for there is a well and nearby what may be the remains of an early stone chapel or baptistery. Little is left of the rectangular building except its low granite walls. It has a raised altar slab at one end and rough stone benches around the inside. In the south-west corner is a trough fed by a stream of clear water, supposedly once used for baptisms.

A little distance away around the well the bushes and trees are festooned with strips of material and pieces of paper as intercessory tokens and offerings to the Goddess. This custom was once widespread throughout Scotland, Wales and Ireland, where *clootie* or cloth wells were common.

*You have heard of the Holy Well, my love*
*On Cuthbert's storied ground,*
*The cloister'd cave all dark above,*
*The cold waves moaning round.*
*Plunge those you love in that Sacred Well*
*At moonlight's mystic hour —*
*They say that sin shall pass therein,*
*The Fiend will lose his power.*

from "The Monk Rock" by R. S. Hawker

Cuthbert here is not the saint of Lindisfarne but probably the Welsh Gwbert, or Cubert. There is a village named after him near Newquay on the north Cornish coast, and the holy well mentioned is in a cave at nearby Holywell Bay.

The theme of water was frequently used by Jesus to communicate deep truths to his disciples. It often represents the psyche or soul, that which clothes the spirit and is the part that remains after death. Our physical bodies come into the world through the waters of birth in the womb, and Christians are formally initiated into the spiritual life through the waters of baptism.

Jesus answered, 'I tell you the truth, no one can enter the kingdom of God unless he is born of water and the Spirit.'

Gospel of St John (ch. 3, v. 5)

In the Western Isles a new-born child was baptized almost immediately by the nurse, who sprinkled three drops of water on the baby's head. This was called the "birth baptism" or "knee-woman's baptism". The clerical baptism took place eight days later, when the child was received into the Church and the Christian faith. The first drop was in the name of the Father and was for

The waters of
baptism, Madron,
Cornwall.

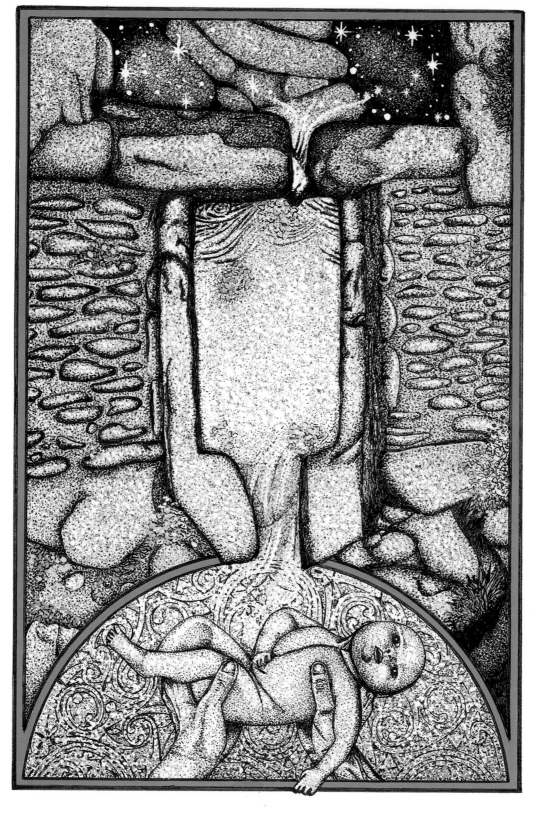

wisdom, the second drop was for the Son and for peace, and the third drop was for the Holy Spirit and for purity. Thus the child was dedicated to the Trinity.

> *The little drop of the Father*
> *On thy little forehead, beloved one.*

> *The little drop of the Son*
> *On thy little forehead, beloved one.*

> *The little drop of the Spirit*
> *On thy little forehead, beloved one.*

> *To aid thee, to guard thee,*
> *To shield thee, to surround thee.*

> from the *Carmina Gadelica* (iii, 17)

If a child died unbaptized, it was not allowed to be buried in consecrated ground, hence the urgency of the first ceremony. It was believed that such an unfortunate child had no soul, although it did have a spirit. The first water in which the new-born infant was washed had a gold or silver coin placed in it to ensure the good fortune and health of the child, and suitable prayers and incantations accompanied this process as well. Nine palmfuls of water were poured on to the baby.

These days we usually take for granted the water in our homes, and expect an immediate and constant flow. Only when there is a drought and restrictions are imposed are we reminded that it can become scarce and should not be wasted. It is a precious resource to be valued and not polluted with chemicals and the effluent of factories or sewers. Our present society tends to regard water as a commodity to be exploited, along with the rest of the earth's natural resources. If we are to follow the example of the Celts, then we must learn to respect and protect our water, and realize that our life depends on preserving its purity and conserving its supply.

The Celts, both pagan and Christian, knew that water was vital to life and was to be used wisely and enjoyed; they valued and understood its worth. This image of the River of Life found in the Book of Revelation would have inspired them:

> Then the angel showed me the river of the water of life, as clear as crystal, flowing from the throne of God and of the Lamb down the middle of the great street of the city.

> Book of Revelation (ch. 22, vv. 1, 2a)

# A·P·R·I·L

*God guide me with Thy wisdom,*
*God chastise me with Thy justice,*
*God help me with Thy mercy,*
*God protect me with Thy strength.*

*God fill me with Thy fullness,*
*God shield me with Thy shade,*
*God fill me with Thy grace*
*For the sake of Thine Anointed Son.*

*Jesu Christ of the seed of David,*
*Visiting One of the Temple,*
*Sacrificial Lamb of the Garden,*
*Who died for me.*

from the *Carmina Gadelica* (i, 65)

*E*ASTER occurs in April more often than not. It is a season of rejoicing after the rigours and austerity of Lent, but it is also a time when the themes of justice, sacrifice, mercy and grace are to the fore. The date of Easter is closely linked to the Jewish Passover and is calculated from the moon's phases, being the first Sunday after the full moon following the spring equinox.

One of the contentious issues which precipitated the Synod of Whitby in 664 CE was the method of dating Easter. The Celtic churches disagreed with the continental practice and resisted pressure to adopt the Roman custom that was common throughout the rest of Europe. The Alexandrian method had been formally adopted by Rome in 525 CE, but the Celtic churches had not accepted

this. The King of Northumbria, Oswy, had been converted by monks from Lindisfarne, while his wife, Queen Eanfleda, who was from Kent, was used to the Roman way and so they rarely celebrated Easter together. Although this issue was a catalyst for the synod, it was really about who should exercise ultimate power and authority. It took place at Whitby and was presided over by St Hilda in the double monastery founded by her there.

Bishop Colman of Lindisfarne represented the Celtic interest, while Agilbet, aided by the Anglo-Saxon Wilfrid, a clever and eloquent man, spoke for the opposing side. He ridiculed the Celts, disparaged St Columba and claimed the authority of St Peter himself to support his case, namely, that the whole Western world conformed to the Roman ideas. Consequently in 669 CE Archbishop Theodore ruled in favour of Rome and imposed their conventions on the Celtic churches. Following their defeat, the Lindisfarne contingent withdrew and the community divided. Colman went back to Iona, accompanied by many of the monks, but eventually returned to his native Ireland and established a monastery on the island of Inishboffin.

Iona is a small island just off the coast of the island of Mull in the Inner Hebrides. With the Atlantic Ocean to the west, the island appears to be on the very edge of civilization. In fact it occupies a pivotal position in the seaways along this coast of the British Isles and is well placed for contact with the Highlands and islands of Scotland, as well as Ireland, and further south to Wales, Cornwall and Brittany.

It is only about 3 miles long and 1 mile wide and was formerly known as the Island of the Druids, showing that it was a significant centre of knowledge and spiritual matters long before the Christian faith took root.

The word Iona means "dove" in Hebrew and it is strange that Columba, the island's most famous son, means "dove" in Latin. The dove is the Christian symbol of the Holy Spirit and is particularly associated with the festival of Pentecost, which occurs seven weeks after Easter. Legend tells us that St Columba landed on 12 May 563 CE, which was the eve of Pentecost that year.

This followed his self-imposed exile from Ireland after the battle of Cuildrevne, for which he had been responsible. As a penance, when he and his companions reached the island, he climbed a nearby hill to make sure he could not see his native country. This spot is known today as Cairn of the Back Turned to Ireland. It was his experience of being involved in dispute and bloodshed which led him to establish a monastery on Iona as a base for spreading the Christian message of hope and peace.

St Columba died in 597 CE. A century later in 697 CE, Adamnan, the ninth abbot of Iona, who wrote a Life of St Columba, convened an international meeting in Ireland which was attended by fifty-one rulers and forty leading churchmen. At this gathering he persuaded them to adopt "The Law of Innocents", which forbade injury to the elderly, clergy, and women and children in wartime. The aim was to protect all non-combatants from indiscriminate slaughter.

In Celtic society, the Druids were the negotiators who had the ability to prevent two sides from coming into conflict, with the authority to intervene before a battle commenced and to stop the opposing armies from engaging in bloodshed. St Columba, Adamnan and the successive abbots of Iona were continuing the tradition which predated the introduction of the Christian faith of seeking to bring peace to people who were often at war with neighbouring tribes and nations. There is a poem attributed to Columba which concludes, "My Druid is Christ, the Son of God." Perhaps there are echoes of Christ's mediating role between God and man here.

Blessed are the peacemakers, for they will be called Sons of God.

Gospel of St Matthew (ch. 5, v. 9)

The abbey is the largest and most prominent building on Iona. Most of its stonework is medieval and was partly restored by the Church of Scotland between 1902 and 1910. It is now used for services by members of the Iona Community, founded by George MacLeod in 1938. He left Govan on Clydeside with twelve companions, some of whom were ministers and some craftsmen, with the intention of rebuilding the remaining secular parts of the abbey. The long restoration process was finally completed in 1967, when at the age of seventy-two he retired as leader of the Community.

It was his intention not only to repair the fabric of the buildings, as a sign of faith in the old monastic ideal of labour and prayer, but to create a spiritual centre from which members of the Community and visitors could return to their own local areas and places of work, refreshed in their Christian vision and vocation. Today the Iona Community welcomes visitors and pilgrims from all over the world. It has a deep concern for young people and their welfare, and offers many courses through the summer months. It would seem that Columba's ancient prophecy of Iona as a place of the spirit is being fulfilled.

*Iona of my heart,*
*Iona of my love,*
*Instead of monks' voices*
*Shall be the lowing of cattle;*
*But ere the world come to an end,*
*Iona shall be as it was.*

Every Monday evening, during worship in the abbey church on Iona, the Community takes as its theme the concerns of peace and justice. As a body they have a commitment to these values and express this both in intercession and in their activities in local communities and internationally. They consider prayer and action to be, as they put it, two sides of the same coin.

Years ago in this part of Scotland, before a man or woman attended a

court of law or faced judgement of any kind, having fasted they would go at first light to a stream which marked a boundary and which subsequently divided into three separate flows. Here they would bathe their face three times, using water from the junction of the streams, and afterwards let the sun shine upon it. During this ritual a suitable incantation for justice was recited.

> *The hand of God keeping me,*
> *The love of Christ in my veins,*
> *The strong Spirit bathing me,*
> *The Three shielding and aiding me.*

from the *Carmina Gadelica* (iv, 145)

This ceremony was a symbolic act, each part of it having a particular significance. The water and the activity of washing were for purification; the confluence of the three streams represented the union of the Trinity, the Father, Son and Holy Spirit; and the warming influence of the morning sun, heavenly grace.

The stone high crosses are much older than the abbey and five early examples survive on Iona. The three which stand out in the open are to the west of the abbey, near the site of the original foundation. It is unclear when they were carved and they could date from the middle of the eighth century to the early tenth century.

The finest of these and the best preserved is St Martin's Cross. Made of red granite and standing nearly 17 feet tall, it is richly decorated with bosses and serpents. The Virgin Mary and child, Daniel in the lions' den and Abraham's sacrifice of Isaac are carved on the west side. Adamnan, Columba's biographer, tells us that St Martin of Tours, after whom the cross is named, was mentioned in the liturgy used on Iona during St Columba's lifetime.

The second, St John's Cross, is a replica, as the eighth-century original is undergoing repair. Again it is decorated with bosses and serpents, scrolls and interlaced knots. Only part of the sandstone shaft of the third one, St Matthew's Cross, remains on its granite base. On one side it shows the temptation of Adam and Eve in the Garden of Eden. There is no representation of the crucified Christ on any of these crosses. They tell the Easter story and are empty, for Christ is risen.

A later monument called Maclean's Cross, which dates from the late fifteenth century, marks the place where St Columba rested and the white horse bade him farewell on the final day of his earthly life.

On the way from the abbey to the arable land called the Machair on the west coast of the island, the pilgrim passes Sithean Mór or the Great Mound of the Fairies, which was a site of pre-Christian revelling. One day St Columba climbed to the top of this little green knoll and stretched out his hands in prayer to heaven, whereupon angels appeared. In later days pilgrims and local people would gather here at Michaelmas in September for celebration, hoping

Iona Abbey, St
Martin's Cross and
St John's Cross.

to see St Michael, the Virgin Mary and St Columba. The place is now known as the Hill of the Angels.

Dùn-I at 332 feet is the highest point of the island and in a sheltered place on the northern side, well hidden by rocks, is the Well of the Age, also known as the Well of Eternal Youth. Pilgrims would come to this small, triangular well at dawn to touch its healing water just as the rising sun reflected on its surface. Through this they hoped to regain physical strength or even to recapture the dreams and aspirations of their younger days, the visions of their youth.

The circular remains of a hermit's cell can be found at the foot of the southern slopes of Dùn-I. It is thought by some to have been one of the places where St Columba withdrew for prayer.

On the way from the ferry to the abbey are the ruins of a Benedictine nunnery. It was established at the beginning of the thirteenth century and the chapel was at one time the burial-place of distinguished women in this part of Scotland. What remains of the cloister has been made into a quiet garden for visitors and pilgrims to enjoy and for rest. The restored St Ronan's Chapel stands on the north side of the ruined nunnery and is now a small museum housing many carved stones from the island.

*The peace of joys,*
*The peace of lights,*
*The peace of consolations.*

*The peace of souls,*
*The peace of heaven,*
*The peace of virgins.*

*The peace of the fairy bowers,*
*The peace of peacefulness,*
*The peace of everlasting.*

from the *Carmina Gadelica* (iii, 269)

None of the buildings on Iona date back to Columba's time, but St Oran's Chapel, which stands in the middle of the graveyard called Reilig Odhrain, is the oldest structure on the island, dating from the twelfth century. It was built by Somerled, Lord of the Isles, and was a burial-place for his successors until the sixteenth century. There are said to be sixty kings buried in Reilig Odhrain, forty-eight of them Scottish, eight Norwegian and four Irish. According to Shakespeare, King Duncan, who was murdered by Macbeth, was carried here for burial.

After St Columba's burial here the place was regarded as a sanctuary for those fleeing from oppression. A fugitive was safe once within the confines of Reilig Odhrain and the monastic community would take responsibility and care for the person until justice was obtained.

The practice of sanctuary is found in many of the stories of the Celtic saints in which they protected not only their fellow humans but also wild creatures. Christian sanctuaries were recognized by Roman law towards the end of the fourth century CE through the acknowledgement of the authority of a bishop as a confessor, and during the fifth century CE these privileges were extended to church buildings and their surrounds. This continued until 1623, when James I abolished the privilege of sanctuary for criminals, although it wasn't until 100 years later that it was withdrawn for civil offences.

Pennant Melangell is a hidden place nestling in the rounded Berwyn Hills, at the head of the Tanat Valley in Powys, mid-Wales. The large, enclosed churchyard with its ancient yew trees calls to mind the right of sanctuary attributed to this place. It is thought that there was a nunnery here, rather than a monastic settlement, founded by St Melangell, a seventh-century princess who initially chose to live here alone.

She has a special association with hares, known locally as "Melangell's little lambs". This came about because Prince Brochwel was hunting these animals in the valley one day when he came across the saint kneeling in a dense thicket in prayer, with a hare sheltering in the folds of her garment for protection. Although he urged them on, his hounds refused to pursue the creature and turned back howling. He learned that she had lived alone in the place for fifteen years and had fled from the court of her father Iowchel, an Irish king, to avoid an undesired marriage. The prince was so impressed with Melangell's sanctity that he granted the land to her, with the privilege of perpetual sanctuary. She remained in the valley for a further thirty-seven years, founding a nunnery.

> *They call me a saint,*
> *They bless me and the hares they call my lambs,*
> *Here, in quietness of forest, fastness*
> *of mountain wall . . .*
>
> *My hares, my lambs,*
> *Are sweet velvet nutmegs . . .*
>
> Glenda Beagan

Within living memory the local people would not shoot the hare and still today if one is seen in the vicinity it is customary to shout the blessing "God and Melangell be with you", to ensure its well-being. The animal was sacred to the early Britons and had religious significance for the pre-Christian Celts too.

In the little church which now stands on the site, there is a wooden roodscreen, dating from the fifteenth century, which has recently been re-assembled and restored. In its delicate carving the legend of Melangell and the hare can be traced among the elaborate trails of foliage. In the apsidal east end of the church, called Cell-y-Bedd, meaning "Cell of the Grave", where the saint's

remains were originally interred, the outline of the grave can be seen, marked by stones.

Parts of the shrine containing Melangell's bones date from about 1160, making it the earliest surviving Romanesque shrine in northern Europe. It was restored to its present state in the late 1980s. Around St Melangell's feast day at the end of May, a festival of worship and music is held each year. There has been a great revival of interest in her in recent years.

Pilgrims through the ages have found their way to this isolated place and they still come today for the healing of body, mind and spirit which this sacred site offers. It is a wild place but a place of deep peace; a place that George MacLeod might have described as "very thin", as he did Iona: that is, where

. . . heaven and earth come close together, here the small and the frightened find shelter and hope.

from a prayer by A. M. Allchin

Romanesque shrine, Pennant Melangell, Powys.

Pennant Melangell church, Powys.

The Old Testament often mentions the need to care for strangers or refugees, people who for a variety of reasons and through no fault of their own find themselves homeless or in a foreign land. Today there are many such displaced peoples and asylum seekers. Voluntary exile is rare. More often it is forced upon people, and some form of protection or sanctuary is necessary to maintain dignity and sustain hope. Throughout the Middle Ages, churches retained the legal right of sanctuary whereby a person was protected for a year and a day. Iona and Pennant Melangell remind us of the need to fulfil the timeless role of defending the weak and providing a haven of peace and security for the vulnerable.

Visitors to Iona are usually impressed by the beauty and tranquillity of the island, and the calm surroundings help the pilgrim to focus on and to find an inner peace. Just as external peace is not only an absence of war, conflict and hatred, so inner peace is not just a lack of turmoil and anger. Rather, it is a positive sense of wholeness and well-being, when we are in harmony with our true selves – the Hebrew *shalom*. It is not easy to cultivate this quality and to find the still centre of our lives in the rush and bustle of ordinary life. It doesn't happen by accident, and we need to make space and time to discover this inner wholeness, away from the pressures of daily living. This is not escapism; it requires commitment and means learning how to listen to our own inner voice. Sometimes this can be quite disturbing, as we uncover aspects of our character which we did not know were there and which may surprise or shock us. This dark side of ourselves, those parts of our personalities which we don't allow others to see, may be buried deep within. We shall not find our inner peace until we recognize these features, accept them, and learn to open ourselves to the presence of God's forgiveness, love and the spirit of resurrection.

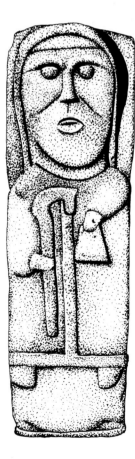

*Deep peace of the running wave to you,*
*Deep peace of the flowing air to you,*
*Deep peace of the quiet earth to you,*
*Deep peace of the shining stars to you,*
*Deep peace of the Son of Peace to you.*

Fiona Macleod

Stone figures at White Island, County Fermanagh.

# M·A·Y

### Beltane Blessing

*The cross of Christ be our shield down today,*
*The cross of Christ our shield upon our way,*
*The cross of Christ round be our shield and stay,*
*Taking at our hands the blessing of May*
   *At our hands blessing of the Beltane Day.*

  from *Poems of the Western Highlanders*

*B*ELTANE, 1 May, is the third Celtic fire festival and the beginning of the light half of the year, whereas Samhain, six months earlier, heralded the dark half. It is a time of growth and expansion as the sun moves towards its peak at the summer solstice in June. For the pastoral Celts, the cattle and sheep which had been kept inside or close to the farmsteads during the long winter months could now be turned out into the fields or taken away to their summer pastures.

  Samhain was overlaid by All Saints' Day and All Souls' Day, Imbolc by the feast of St Bridget and Candlemas, and Lughnasad, on 1 August, by Lammas, but somehow the Church never subdued the raw, primal energy of Beltane. It has had no major Christian festival grafted on to it. The feast of the Apostles St Philip and St James is celebrated on this day, but it is not as widely known or as popular as May Day.

  Perhaps because of this, the whole month of May is regarded as the Virgin Mary's month and is dedicated to her. The hawthorn, also called "may", is her flower, and until the changes to our modern calendar in 1752, it would have come into blossom at Beltane, whereas now the flowers are seen towards the end of the month. The Druids considered the tree to be unlucky, even though it was connected with this festival and dedicated to the Goddess. Medicinally, it is a plant that has a quality of balancing, with the ability to either stimulate or depress the heart, causing both low and high blood pressures to reach more normal levels.

*May-day, season fair,*
*perfect time of year,*
*the blackbird's song a poem,*
*to the sun's first slender ray.*

Irish, ninth century

The name Beltane comes from Bel, who was a solar deity, and *tane*, meaning fire; hence it was celebrated with fire and light. In pagan times the kindling of a Beltane fire served a number of purposes. It was a means of destroying malign influences by purifying the air, thus ensuring that people, homes and animals would be protected. It also safeguarded the continued fertility of both the community and its livestock.

The fires were built on hilltops, using only sacred woods, and lit at daybreak as the sun rose. Each fire was made in two sections with a passage down the middle, and all was enclosed within a circular trench representing the sun. The spark to light the fire was created from the friction of two planks of oak. When the blaze was established, the whole community walked sunwise around the fire three times. After this the cattle were herded three times through the narrow gap between the two fires to ensure their health. When the fire had died down, the sick animals were driven across the embers, and then the people would sprinkle each other with the sacred ash and blacken their faces. Finally, torches were lit and the young men first circled the herds to ask for their safety and fertility, then their fields of growing crops and lastly their dwellings.

Domestic fires, which were kept alight right through the year, had been extinguished on Beltane Eve, 30 April, in readiness to be rekindled from these torches next day, and they would again be kept burning for the whole year. These rituals were presided over by the Druids, but the element of fire retained its importance after their power had waned. As in common with many ancient peoples, the hearthstone was almost thought of as the altar of the house, a focal point which provided light and warmth, and enabled the food to be cooked. The Celtic Christians of the Scottish Highlands and Islands had prayers for each small task associated with the labour of keeping the fire alight and tended. All was related to the god who provided fire for their use. Turf or peat was cut for fuel in rectangular blocks, dried and then stacked near the house. "Lifting" the peats was the first household duty of the day for the woman of the house, when the fire was coaxed into life once more.

*I will kindle my fire this morning*
*In presence of the holy angels of heaven . . .*

*God, kindle Thou in my heart within*
*A flame of love to my neighbour.*

from the *Carmina Gadelica* (i,231)

It was taboo to turn a peat block so that the burning side was uppermost in the fire, and also for a woman to fan the flames with her apron or skirt. These beliefs stemmed from a story, well known in the Western Isles, which relates that when Jesus was about to be crucified there were no nails to put through his hands and feet, and no bellows with which to blow the fire to make them. The blacksmith refused to co-operate for such a purpose. A tinker woman offered to fan the flames with her skirt and a tinker forged the iron nails, turning the peats over as he did so. It was said that as a punishment for their ill-deed, tinkers and their families were condemned to wander, travelling from place to place without rest, for eternity.

Smothering or *smooring* the peats to keep the fire in overnight was the final task of the day. This took the form of a little ceremony where the embers were raked evenly into a circle on the hearthstone. They were then divided into three equal sections, leaving a small heap of glowing embers in the middle. A peat block was laid between each section, with the ends resting on the central pile. The first peat was placed in position in the name of the God of Life, the second in the name of the God of Peace, and the third in the name of the God of Grace. The whole was then covered with ashes in the name of the Three of Light, so that the fire was subdued but not put out. The raised central portion was known as "the Hearth of the Three". When the *smooring* had been accomplished, a prayer such as the following was intoned:

*The sacred Three*
*To save,*
*To shield,*
*To surround,*
*The hearth,*
*The house,*
*The household,*
*This eve,*
*This night,*
*Oh! this eve,*
*This night,*
*And every night,*
*Each single night.     Amen.*

from the *Carmina Gadelica* (i, 235)

Despite its emphasis on female fertility and birth, Beltane was a celebration of the union of the earth goddess and her male consort: that is, the balance of female and male energy, not only in a sexual way but spiritually and emotionally too. Getting the balance right is important for the health and well-being both of individuals and of society as a whole. It is equally unhealthy for the feminine to dominate as for the patriarchal to prevail. Interdependence and balance are the lessons here.

This concept was embodied in the double monasteries founded by people such as St Bridget and St Hilda. Here men and women lived in separate accommodation but shared a common concern for the welfare of the whole community. In practical ways double monasteries had considerable advantages, as the male and female members could complement each other with a sensible division of labour, according to natural strength and skill. Women might use their talents in sewing and weaving, both for ecclesiastical vestments and for everyday clothing. They could wash and repair the altar linen and attend to the beauty and cleanliness of the church and monastic buildings. For their part, the men would do the more strenuous manual work, such as building, digging, clearing the ground and ploughing. They could also provide protection and, in those days of a solely male priesthood, clergy to administer the sacraments. However, the overall authority within a double monastery often resided with an abbess who governed both the male and the female houses. As mentioned above, St Hilda, a disciple of St Aidan, ruled over a double monastery, at Whitby, and so did St Ebba, at Coldingham in Scotland.

Double monasteries were also founded on the continent of Europe in France, Italy and Spain. However, they did not become the norm and, with the rise in the power of the Roman Church, were eventually superseded by single-sex religious houses.

There has been a revival of interest in Christian communities where men and women can work more closely together. A contemporary Celtic example is the non-residential Community of Aidan and Hilda, based near Stratford-upon-Avon in Warwickshire. This community aims to help its members develop a personal way of life through the inspiration and example of the Celtic saints.

A short distance from the main road running between Dublin and Belfast lies the monastic enclosure of St Buithe, called Mainistir Buithe, or Monasterboice. This saint made a pilgrimage to Rome and travelled through Scotland on his return to Ireland. Here he raised the dying Nectan, King of the Picts, and founded several monasteries, including Kirkbuddo, meaning "church of Buithe". His Irish settlement was for both men and women, and was therefore similar to the double monastery of his contemporary St Bridget at Kildare.

However, to avoid the possibility of scandal, the two houses of his community were placed some distance apart. Rules for the conduct of double

monasteries had been drawn up by St Basil and his sister St Macrina in Asia Minor, modern Turkey, in the fourth century CE, and to prevent unnecessary distractions the two parts of their monastery were located on opposite sides of a river.

Monasterboice draws many thousands of visitors each year, tourists and pilgrims alike, who come to see the monuments in the small churchyard on the site of St Buithe's early monastery. Although it is not as impressive as the one at Glendalough, there is here a ninth-century round tower which was damaged by fire in 1097 and has lost its top section. There are also two ruined churches, one of which dates from the eighth or ninth century, and an ancient stone sundial or mass clock, marked with the canonical hours, which would have helped pilgrims to observe the correct times for their devotions and prayers.

The carved stone crosses here are reputed to be the finest in Ireland, and the subjects portrayed on them are similar to those on other crosses at Durrow and Clonmacnois, also in Ireland, and on the high crosses on Iona in Scotland. The numerous stone panels are richly carved with figures and scriptural subjects. Biblical scenes on the theme of deliverance are depicted, such as Noah escaping the Flood, Isaac being saved from the sword of his father Abraham, Daniel surviving the lions' den, and the three young Hebrew men walking unharmed in the fiery furnace. Many events from the life of Christ are also shown, and here the early Celtic Christians would have been able to read in stone the whole story of their faith: of the creation, mankind's fall, the Jewish prophets, kings and judges, the means of salvation, judgement, hell and heaven. Three crosses still stand in the enclosure although there were probably more at one time.

Muiredach's Cross or the South Cross is 17 feet tall and exceptionally detailed and well preserved. It has an inscription on the base which reads, "A prayer for Muiredach, under whose auspices this cross was made." Both it and the West Cross have stone caps on top, shaped like a little house or oratory, with gable finials at either end of the roof. These are reminiscent of the wooden buildings which would have been familiar to the sculptors of the crosses. Portable metalwork reliquaries, such as the eighth-century Monymusk Shrine now in the National Museum in Edinburgh, were made in this shape too.

The majestic West Cross or Tall Cross, standing over 20 feet high, has twenty-two sculptured panels and, like Muiredach's Cross, it is almost un-damaged. Sadly, only the head and part of the upper shaft of the North Cross have survived. It is not as highly ornamented as the other two, but it has a carving of the Crucifixion on the west side.

Monasterboice, unlike most monasteries of the day, appears to have escaped the ravages of the Norsemen, and its decline began only with the construction of the neighbouring Cistercian monastery at Mellifont in the twelfth century.

*Opposite*:
Muiredach's Cross, Monasterboice, County Louth.

*O upright and renowned judge*
*Whose hands are bright*
*With shining deeds*
*O Buithe, good son of Bronagh*
*Come to my help each day.*

Irish, twelfth-century copy of *Annals* written
on the death of St Buithe in 521 CE

The art and science of dowsing for earth energies has experienced a marked resurgence in recent decades, and one of the most famous energy lines which has been rediscovered in Britain is known as the St Michael Line, a ley which runs from Carn Lês Boel near Land's End in Cornwall to Hopton-on-Sea on the coast of Norfolk. The sacred sites strung out along this imaginary line are aligned to the sunrise at Beltane, 1 May.

Thanks to the investigations and dedication of contemporary dowsers, it has been shown that this energy line is not straight but, serpent-like, meanders across the land. Also, it has been suggested that there are actually two energy lines running close together across the country from south-west to north-east: one, the so-called Michael Line, represents the male energy and a complementary current named the Mary Line embodies the female energy. At certain axial points these lines cross over each other and powerful energy centres result. These have been compared to the *chakra* points in the human body.

Many of the places on both these lines have links with the early Celtic saints, who may have become the inheritors and keepers of the sacred knowledge identified with these sites, continuing the custodial duties of the Druids. The word "hermit", which was often applied to these holy men and women, may relate to the Greek god Hermes, who was traditionally a guardian of the earth currents.

To make cloth two sets of threads are required, the taut warp threads running the length of the cloth, and the pliable weft thread interwoven backwards and forwards across them. It is this interlacing of the yarn that holds the cloth together and makes it strong and serviceable; the tension and balance of the threads must be correct to make a good cloth. The warp threads have no use without the weft, and vice versa. Again, the theme of interdependence is emphasized.

Until relatively recently, especially in rural areas, making blankets and material for garments was an integral and necessary part of the tasks of each household. There were many stages between shearing the sheep and the final product, and most of the textile processes were traditionally done in the home by the female members of the family. In some places in the Celtic countries this way of life survived into the present century. In the Inner Hebrides and on the mainland of Scotland, men used to do the actual weaving, while in the

Woven pattern.

Balance of male and female.

Outer Hebrides it was mainly the task of the women.

Each stage required patience and care, from sorting and carding the fleece, to dyeing it with plants, spinning the thread, warping the loom, weaving and finally waulking the cloth. This last operation caused the web of threads to mesh together and thickened the cloth. Waulking was a communal activity and three women of great skill and specialist knowledge were invited: one to lead the rhythmic singing which accompanied the work, one to lead the waulking itself and one to make sure that the ceremonies were carried out in the correct order. A song was not allowed to be repeated during the waulking or it would result in misfortune to the singer and the wearer of the cloth. A long, grooved wooden board was set up on trestles with seats arranged down each side, and the web of woven cloth was unrolled. Soaked in warm water, ammonia and soap, it was then worked vigorously from side to side and moved sunwise lengthways at the same time. At the end, as the cloth was folded and smoothed out with the palms of the hands, it was blessed and consecrated in the name of the Trinity.

The Celts' love of bright colour could be expressed to the full in dyeing and weaving:

*Thrums and odds of thread they all must go,*
*My hand never kept them nor will keep;*
*All colours of the shower's arching bow*

*'Neath the cross-stretch through my fingers sweep,*
*Red and madder, white and black they go,*
*Green, dark grey, and scarlet in a row,*
*Colour of the sheep, and roan, and blue,*
*No ends wanting to the clothing due.*

*Calm Bride I pray, open-handed, kind*
*Mary I pray, mild, the loving so,*
*The Christ I pray, Jesu of mankind,*
*That alone to death I may not go,*
*That alone to death I may not go.*

from *Poems of the Western Highlanders*

Of course, no work was carried out on a Sunday, the day of rest, and in Uist, one of the Western Isles, a cross or crucifix was suspended over the loom on Saturday night to protect and bless it until work commenced again on Monday morning. Each Thursday of the week was dedicated to St Columba, and considered to be an auspicious day to undertake any new task; threading the loom or weaving was often started on this day.

*Thursday excelling,*
*For warp and fulling . . .*

from *Poems of the Western Highlanders*

Today on Harris and Lewis the production of tweed is a very important part of the Hebridean economy, and both men and women work at their mechanized looms in sheds and huts, often attached to their homes. There are weaving factories on the islands but it is still largely an individual home-based occupation. Certain exclusive tailors in London have bales of tweed in their shops bearing the names of the respective weavers.

It is vital on our spiritual pilgrimage to maintain a healthy balance between our own thoughts, ideas, perceptions and feelings about our journey, and what may be a very different reality. To be able to have a dialogue with someone else, to have a sounding-board or to check things out, is very useful. Objective comment is necessary or we can become too introspective as we travel alone.

On an outer, physical journey our companions, the weather, shared meals and experience of new places help to keep this balance for us; but in familiar surroundings, where our senses may be a little dull and we are not stimulated by external novelty and change, it is easy to lose our perspective, and indeed our enthusiasm.

The female inner journey needs to be balanced by the male outer journey. One way to overcome these difficulties is to have a spiritual director or someone who can provide advice and insight. In a way, they become the outer journey. Following in the footsteps of the Desert Fathers, the Celts had their soul-friends, close companions who walked the pilgrim path with them and who offered counsel and consolation.

It was the belief that one's soul-friend was a gift from the Holy Spirit, and that the link established was not severed by the death of either of them. Known as *anam-chara* in Gaelic and *periglowr* in Welsh, these intimate comrades, and their wisdom, were much valued. St Comgall of Bangor in Ireland, whose feast day is 11 May, once said, "A man without a soul-friend is a body without a head."

*Father be my friend,*
*And Son be my friend,*
*Spirit be my friend,*
*Three to send and befriend.*

from *Poems of the Western Highlanders*

Figure on a pillar at Cardonagh, County Donegal.

Pilgrim carrying staff and bell, Killadeas, County Fermanagh.

# J·U·N·E

*And did those feet in ancient time*
*Walk upon England's mountains green?*
*And was the holy Lamb of God*
*On England's pleasant pastures seen?*

*And did the Countenance Divine*
*Shine forth upon our clouded hills?*
*And was Jerusalem builded here*
*Among these dark Satanic mills?*

William Blake (1757–1827)

*G*LASTONBURY is so rich in its spiritual heritage, history and atmosphere that it appeals to a very wide variety of pilgrims. It was a religious centre long before the arrival of the Christian faith in Britain, and so traces of the Christian Celtic tradition are layered with the pre-Christian, and later the Saxon, Norman, medieval and New Age additions, and all have become interwoven with each other.

Each year towards the end of June there are both Roman Catholic and Anglican pilgrimages to Glastonbury, when many thousands of people from the south of England process through the streets of the town with banners and attend open-air services in the grounds of the ruined abbey. On the same day as the Anglican pilgrimage, a Greek Orthodox service is held in the undercroft of St Joseph's Chapel when the icon of Our Lady of Glastonbury is venerated. The pilgrimage to Glastonbury was a favoured pursuit in the Middle Ages too, but died out when the abbey was disbanded and destroyed in the 1530s during the Dissolution of the Monasteries, and was only revived in the twentieth century. In 1988 the millennial anniversary of the death of Glastonbury's most famous abbot, St Dunstan, was celebrated. Under his leadership the abbey became a centre for the renewal of disciplined monastic life, a movement which swept through Europe in the tenth century.

June brings Midsummer Day with its long hours of daylight, and the summer solstice, when the sun is at the height of its power. The light has triumphed; yet from this point, when the sun enters the zodiacal sign of Cancer, the wheel turns and the decline into the dark begins again. For the pre-Christian sun-worshipping Celts, this day was one of the highlights of the year, a time of great sanctity and energy, so it is significant that the organized Christian pilgrimages take place at this time. The summit of Glastonbury Tor, rising from the surrounding plain to a height of 500 feet, would have provided a magnificent focus for the midsummer rituals and festivities.

The parish church in the main street is dedicated to St John the Baptist, whose feast is celebrated on Midsummer Day, 24 June. According to the New Testament, he was the forerunner of Christ and came to prepare the way for him. He met his death when, at Salome's request, he was taken from prison and beheaded. In early Celtic times the cult of the head was strong. It was considered to be the seat of power and was regarded as a solar emblem. Thus the patronage of John the Baptist may be linked to these early pre-Christian beliefs. The plant St John's wort was also regarded as an emblem of the sun and was gathered on Midsummer Eve, 23 June, to be made into garlands which were worn or hung up in the home as a talisman.

In Scotland the people believed that St Columba always had some of the plant folded in his clothing because of his devotion to John the Baptist. They would carry pieces in their undergarments, secured under the left armpit, and one of its names was "armpit package of Columba".

*Saint John's wort, Saint John's wort,*
*My envy whosoever has thee,*
*I will pluck thee with my right hand,*
*I will preserve thee with my left hand,*
*Whoso findeth thee in the cattle fold,*
*Shall never be without kine.*

from the *Carmina Gadelica* (ii, 103)

From the summer solstice in June to the winter solstice in December, life withdraws into itself, like a deep breath being taken in, and then from December to June the breath is slowly let out, bringing new life and growth. At the equinoxes in March and September, the breath has reached its half-way point. *Speira*, the Greek word from which spiral is derived, means "coils of a serpent" and this symbol is sometimes used to express this inhalation and exhalation, and also the movement of the sun through the seasons. Circular bosses and also lozenge shapes are used to represent the sun too.

These ideas appear on the carved stones at the Neolithic tumulus of Newgrange in County Meath, the second-oldest building in Europe, which dates from the third millennium BCE, and also on the later stone crosses such as St John's Cross and St Martin's Cross on Iona. Often the winter sun is shown as a tightly coiled clockwise spiral and the summer sun as a looser anti-clockwise coil. The equinoxes appear as an equal double spiral or as evenly matched separate spirals, equinox meaning literally "equal night". The west face of the cross at Kilree in Ireland clearly displays the four states of the sun during the year.

On a gilt bronze plaque found at Athlone which shows Christ on the cross, his breast is covered in conspicuous interwoven spiral forms, possibly re-presenting the rhythms of the breath and the heartbeat. A spiral of the Trinity rises from his head and is evocative of the triple spiral design found on the entrance stone at Newgrange. In the distinctive form known as "the Celtic cross", where a circle surrounds or is superimposed on a four-armed cross, the disc or circle represents the sun, which was the deity of the Druids and other earlier pre-Christian peoples. With the acceptance of Christianity, this sun symbol was transmuted to mean the light of Christ, the Christian sun who rose on Easter Day. Often pagan stones were claimed and reused as the new spirituality was grafted on to the old. In the National Museum of Ireland in Dublin there is a stone pillar removed from Brandon Hill, Arraglen, which shows two swastikas, a Druidic sign for the sun, with an arrow between them pointing upwards. Above the arrow is a Christian cross within a circle, implying that the new light of the world, Christ, had superseded the old ways.

When the Saxons arrived at Glastonbury in 658 CE, during their advance into the south-west peninsula of Britain, they found a settlement and mon-astery of great antiquity. Glastonbury is a Saxon word, but an earlier name for the place was Ynys Witrin, meaning "Isle of Glass". This may be a reference to the fact that Glastonbury was at one time almost surrounded by water, which would have reflected the sky like a mirror. Although it is now an inland area, the surrounding fields having been drained and cultivated, Glastonbury had in common with other sacred places a separateness. It could be reached only by crossing in a boat, or along a narrow causeway. Standing at the top of the Tor, it is not too difficult to imagine a shallow expanse of water covering the countryside and stretching to the distant hills, 10 or 15 miles away.

There are four main sites for the Christian pilgrim in and around the small town: the tor, with the tower of St Michael's Church on the summit; the abbey ruins; the Chalice Well at the foot of the Tor; and on the edge of the town Wearyall Hill and its hawthorn tree. Each of these sites could be a place of pilgrimage in its own right.

The Tor dominates the landscape and is visible for many miles across the Somerset Levels. Long ago its lower slopes were heavily wooded, but now it stands stark and bare, with only the fourteenth-century tower of St Michael's Church on top. On the tower, carvings of St Michael, who is holding a pair of

The Calf of Man
Crucifix,
Glastonbury Tor,
Joseph of
Arimathea and the
entrance stone at
Newgrange,
County Meath.

The Glastonbury
Thorn.

The ruins of
Glastonbury
Abbey.

scales and weighing the souls of the dead, and St Bridget, who is milking a cow, can be seen. An earlier church here was destroyed by an earthquake in 1275, and before this there may have been a hermitage on the site.

A serpentine ritual maze winds its way up the slopes of the Tor, and the entrance to this seven-circuit labyrinth is marked by huge boulders to the south-west, known as the Druid's Stones; these align with the St Michael Line. From the abbey grounds the sun appears to rise over the Tor at two significant times of the year in the Christian calendar: namely, the feast of St Michael, at the end of September, and around mid-March, when St Joseph of Arimathea and St Patrick share a feast day. For medieval pilgrims the Tor may have been used as a Calvary Mount, an idea found throughout Europe, where the Stations of the Cross would be passed at various levels on the ascent. A fourteenth-century bronze pilgrim's badge has been found on the slopes.

The Tor was also long regarded as an entrance to Annwn, the Celtic

Underworld. Often the Celtic Christians built on top of existing pagan sites which were already sacred, and they could also absorb the people's beliefs and blend them into the new faith. However, occasionally the old religions and Druidism were so strong that destruction and exorcism were felt to be necessary. This is evident in the tale of St Collen. He was a seventh-century monk from Wales who, having been abbot for a time, then withdrew to a cell at the foot of the Tor. One day, so the story goes, a messenger appeared at his hut bearing an invitation from Gwynn ap Nudd, the Lord of the Underworld, who lived beneath the Tor, asking him to pay a visit. Collen refused, for it was known that anyone who entered his castle could be enchanted and not return. At the third invitation he consented. In Gwynn's great hall there was feasting and music, and the whole world of faery was displayed before his eyes. Collen scattered the holy water he had brought with him and Gwynn, his castle and the fairy folk vanished at once, leaving the saint alone on the Tor.

The early history of Glastonbury is so shrouded in mystery and uncertainty that we have to rely largely on tradition in piecing together its importance as the birthplace of the Christian faith in Britain. These long-established stories start with Jesus himself, and this is the import of Blake's poem, now known as "Jerusalem", which has become almost a second national anthem in England. They assert that Christ visited Glastonbury as a young man, in the company of his great-uncle Joseph of Arimathea, during the "missing years" of his life which are not accounted for in the Bible and before the start of his public ministry. Joseph was a member of the Jewish Council, the Sanhedrin, and a man of considerable wealth, as shown by the fact that he had a private tomb which he offered for the burial of Jesus. He is thought to have held a position of authority in Britain, overseeing the Roman metal trade in Cornwall and Somerset; thus he would have been familiar with the south-west of Britain and its people. Both these areas have many legends concerning Joseph and Jesus, and their visits to places associated with mining and shipping.

It is said that, after the Crucifixion Joseph returned to Glastonbury in 63 CE with twelve companions, including his son Josephes and Mary, the mother of Jesus. There is documentary evidence that he was commissioned to take the Gospel to Britain by the Apostle St Philip, who himself led a mission to Gaul. They came ashore at Wearyall Hill, which was surrounded by sea and where traces of an ancient wharf have been found. Here he thrust his staff into the ground and it burst into leaf and blossom. On the side of the hill there is a stone slab marking the place where they first rested and a small thorn of a Levantine variety still survives, the original having been destroyed in the seventeenth century by a Puritan who was blinded in the act. The tree, unlike our native species, flowers each year at Christmas and again in the spring. There is a similar thorn in the abbey grounds and another outside St John's Church. Blossoms from the holy thorn are ceremonially cut and sent to the reigning monarch at Christmas each year. Joseph brought with him two phials, containing blood and water which flowed from Jesus' side at the Crucifixion,

when he was pierced with the spear. In the chancel of St John's Church a stained-glass window shows the coat of arms of Joseph of Arimathea, a cross and the two precious cruets.

Joseph was given twelve hides of land by the local ruler, King Arviragus, and here the celebrated wattle church was constructed, the *Ecclesia Vetusta*, surrounded by a circle of twelve huts for them to live in. The church was dedicated to Mary, and thus Glastonbury became the earliest centre of the Marian cult in Britain. In 160 CE a stone building dedicated to Christ, St Peter and St Paul was added, and in 633 CE the Old Church was boarded over and covered with lead to try to preserve it. Today the ruins of the Lady Chapel stand adjacent to its site.

Even though the abbey is ruined, it is still an impressive site, nearly 600 feet in length, and for the pilgrim who is particularly interested in the early Christian Church in Britain there are great riches here. British bishops were always accorded precedence at all Church councils until the fifteenth century, because of the great antiquity of the Church in Britain. Christianity was established here 500 years before the mission of St Augustine in 597 CE.

The Lady Chapel, also called St Joseph's Chapel, has a remarkable crypt, now completely exposed as the upper floor has been removed. On its south side, under an arch, is St Joseph's Well, fed by a spring flowing out of natural rock. At ground level, near the arched south doorway, there is a stone with the words "Jesus, Maria" carved on it, perhaps reminding the pilgrim of these early visitors. As well as the hawthorn tree, there is a walnut tree in the grounds which is supposed to burst into leaf miraculously on St Barnabas' Day, 11 June.

Glastonbury was one of the three religious centres in Britain where a perpetual choir was established, the others being Amesbury, near the pagan centre of Stonehenge, and Llantwit Major in south Wales. Some sources cite Old Sarum, near Salisbury, instead of Amesbury. At these places monks provided a continuous cycle of singing every hour of the day and night. It is not known for certain when the perpetual choirs were instituted, and one suggestion is that the inspiration came from St Martin's community at Tours towards the end of the fourth century.

Christian writers of the second and third centuries CE, such as Tertullian and Origen, refer to the spread of Christianity to Britain and this is confirmed by later British writers, such as the Venerable Bede in the eighth century. He mentions that Lucius, a second-century British king who exercised power within the overall supremacy of the Roman Empire, wrote to the Bishop of Rome, Eleutherius, asking for permission to become a Christian. A twelfth-century writer, Geoffrey of Monmouth, gives more detail about this request. Apparently Christian missionaries had been active in Britain during the second century CE and their message interested Lucius. Bishop Eleutherius sent two teachers called Fagan and Dyfan, both Celts, who converted and baptized the king. It was they who added the oratory of St Peter and St Paul to the Old Church. A large number of the king's subjects followed his example and became Christians, and also many pagan temples were replaced with Christian churches. Bishops and archbishops were appointed, and this led to further missionary expansion. Lucius died in Gloucester and was buried in London, though unfortunately he had no heirs to continue his work. There is a tradition that he built churches in Glastonbury, London and Llandaff. His Glastonbury church may have been situated on the former pagan site at the summit of the Tor, where the Celts worshipped the sun-god Bel, the Baal of the Old Testament.

The Chalice Well lies in a peaceful garden between the softly rounded Chalice Hill and the steeper Tor. Although the source of the spring is unknown, it probably rises from the nearby Mendip Hills to the north. The actual well-head is at the top of the long garden, sheltered by trees, and is constructed of two stone chambers filled with clear water. A wooden well-cover was donated in 1919 to give thanks for the end of the First World War, and the design on it is based on a thirteenth-century pattern. It shows two interlinked circles pierced by a lance which holds in balance the two worlds of the visible and invisible, the conscious and the unconscious, the masculine and the feminine. The mandorla formed in the centre is shaped like a fish, the Christian symbol for Christ, hence the name *vesica piscis*. The sacred geometry of the town of Glastonbury is also based on this design of the circles. Because it is a chalybeate well, the water is impregnated with iron and causes a red stain on the rocks and stones over which it flows. The other name for this water source is the Blood Spring. Due to its high mineral content, the water has a very distinctive taste, and lower down the gardens at the Lion's Head Fountain the pilgrim is invited to sample it.

Further descent leads to a small, enclosed paved area called King Arthur's Courtyard. Here is one of the axial points where the Michael Line and the Mary Line cross and there is a pool where pilgrims used to bathe in the healing waters. At the foot of the garden the stream cascades down an attractive waterfall into a shallow pool formed of two overlapping circles, repeating the design on the well-cover. Ancient yew trees grow in the garden here and in Celtic tradition these were associated with death and rebirth. Remarkable for its unfailing flow and constant temperature, the well, which is orientated towards the summer solstice sunrise, saved the town from severe drought in the early 1920s. The Chalice Well Trust, founded in 1958, maintains this place of deep peace and sanctity so that all may come to share in its special atmosphere.

As well as the Blood Spring, there is also the Well House Spring, which rises underground on the Tor and emerges on the opposite side of Well House Lane to the Chalice Well. It leaves a heavy, white calcium deposit on stone, and is also known as the White Spring. These colours, red and white, remind us of the cruets of blood and water that Joseph of Arimathea brought to Glastonbury from the Crucifixion.

Throughout its long history Glastonbury claims links with very many

famous and worthy people, and, among the Celtic saints, Patrick, Bridget and David. After being ordained as a bishop in Gaul, St Patrick came here to seek support and inspiration before starting his missionary work in Ireland. Later in life he returned as abbot to encourage and develop the small Celtic community started in the second century by St Fagan and St Dyfan near the Chalice Well. He died here and was buried on the south side of the altar in the abbey. St Columba is reputed to have visited St Patrick's grave in 504 CE. In the grounds of the abbey is a quiet chapel for prayer and contemplation dedicated to Patrick. It contains some lovely tapestry kneelers with Celtic designs in the Irish colours of green and yellow.

Another church in the town, now wrongly attributed to St Benedict, was at one time dedicated to Patrick's disciple Benignus, who reputedly abandoned his Irish bishopric and, following his master's example, came to die in Glastonbury. He was buried at Mere, where the Abbot's Fish House still stands, until in 901 CE his body was moved to the abbey.

As for St Bridget, there is no reliable evidence that she ever left Ireland, but William of Malmesbury, who is also the source of information about St Patrick, tells us that she visited in 488 CE, soon after St Patrick's death. She settled at Beckery, also called Little Ireland, to the south-west of Glastonbury, and founded a nunnery on Wearyall Hill. On her return to Ireland she is said to have left behind a little bag, a necklace, a small handbell and some weaving implements. These relics were venerated until the Reformation, when they vanished. It is possible that the tradition of her visit grew up because of the large numbers of Irish pilgrims who came to the area to visit the chapel dedicated to St Bride at Beckery.

The eleventh-century *Life of St David* by Rhigyfarch mentions that he also came to Glastonbury and built a church here. William of Malmesbury tells us that he came from Wales with seven bishops, intending to dedicate the Old Church. The night before the event he had a vision of Jesus, who told him that the church had already been dedicated long ago by himself in honour of his mother, Mary, and that it was unseemly to rededicate it. Accordingly, David built an addition to the existing church instead, and at one time there was a brass plate fastened to a pillar telling his story and marking the boundary between the Old Church and his new part. He dedicated this to St Peter and St Paul, as the original oratory, built in 160 CE, had since become the main church. Interestingly, their feast day, 29 June, is close to Midsummer Day. There is a legend that St David's remains were moved from the cathedral of St David's in Wales to Glastonbury in about 960 CE, but as most churches and religious houses in the Middle Ages liked to boast of having important relics, because it was good for revenue, this is uncertain.

The Glastonbury Zodiac, some 30 miles in circumference, is an enormous "temple of the stars" laid out in the landscape, delineated by roads, rivers, hills and other natural features. It has been suggested that the pilgrim, Christian or otherwise, would come here to be instructed in mysteries and hidden knowledge. The Tor forms the head of the Aquarius figure, which here is a phoenix or eagle, and not the more familiar human water-carrier. Both these birds are symbols of resurrection, and appropriately the Chalice Well is situated on the tip of the bird's beak, speaking of the rebirth experienced in initiation and the finding of new wisdom.

Glastonbury was even called Roma Secunda, the second Rome, because of its importance and influence. By drawing together so many strands of the Christian faith in Britain, it has, over the last 2,000 years, created in visitors a deep impression and given lasting inspiration. The diversity of Glastonbury's religious heritage is seen in the different shops in the town, with their mixture of Christian, pagan and New Age items and books for sale. The question of the relationship between the Christian faith and other faiths is never far away, and for the Christian this could be unsettling and puzzling. In a sense, Glastonbury reflects the reality of the wider society in which we live, where different religions, both Eastern and Western, coexist, and a variety of cultures influence and affect each other in our towns and cities. Hopefully, through this proximity, we learn to honour other people's truths and respect the things that are of value to them. The Christian can learn much from the study of other religions, and may at the same time discover more of the essential message of love embodied in the Christian faith.

Two pilgrims on a stone pillar at Cardonagh, County Donegal.

# J·U·L·Y

*O King of stars!*
*Whether my house be dark or bright,*
*Never shall it be closed against any one,*
*Lest Christ close His house against me.*

*If there be a guest in your house*
*And you conceal aught from him,*
*'Tis not the guest that will be without it,*
*But Jesus, Mary's Son.*

translated from the Irish by Kuno Meyer

*I*N THE CHURCH CALENDAR there is a long period during the summer between Pentecost and Advent. Pentecost was originally a Jewish agricultural festival for celebrating the start of the wheat harvest on the fiftieth day after the feast of the Passover. For the Christian Church, the Jewish Passover became Good Friday and Easter, followed seven weeks later by the feast of Pentecost, which is when the Holy Spirit was given to the first disciples in Jerusalem. In this way, what started as a fertility and agricultural festival was transformed into a festival of the Spirit. The original title was retained and the name Pentecost is now used not only for this feast but also for the whole season until Advent Sunday in November or December.

In other Church calendars the Sunday immediately following Pentecost is called Trinity Sunday and the ensuing period is alternatively called the Trinity season. This festival affirms the distinctive Christian belief in one God and three persons: Father, Son and Holy Spirit. The apparent numerical contradiction of this doctrine did not seem to bother the Celts. They had little difficulty in believing in a god who was One-in-Three and Three-in-One, because they were used to the threefold pattern of wisdom and teaching of the Druids. According to the Druidic Triads:

> There are three things which keep order and system in the world: number, weight, and measure.

> Three things which we cannot control: time, space, and truth.

> Three things good as servants, bad as masters: water, fire, and wind.

The basic Druidic belief was in a Trinity, and three golden rays of light representing the three aspects of the godhead were the emblem of Druidism. Duw was the overall god of light who pervaded the universe, and his three aspects were Beli, the creator of the universe as regards the past; Taran, the controlling provident spirit of the present; and Yesu, the coming Saviour of the future. Thus Druidism foreshadowed Christianity. This symbol can be seen today on the banner of the Cornish Gorseth, a gathering of bards held each year in September.

One story tells how St Patrick used the shamrock plant, with its three leaves on one stem, to explain the concept of the Trinity to the High King's daughters in Connacht, and of course it has become the emblem of the Irish nation.

> *Thou shamrock of foliage,*
> *Thou shamrock entwining,*
> *Thou shamrock of the prayer,*
> *Thou shamrock of my love.*

> *Thou shamrock of my sorrow,*
> *Plant of Patrick of the virtues,*
> *Thou shamrock of the Son of Mary,*
> *Journey's-end of the peoples.*

> *Thou shamrock of grace,*
> *Of joy, of the tombs,*
> *It were my wish in death*
> *Thou should'st grow on my grave.*

> from the *Carmina Gadelica* (iv, 139)

The Celts, therefore, provided a stark contrast to the Christian peoples of the Mediterranean, who were influenced by Greek rational thought, and where the Church's teachers wrestled with language and concepts for centuries before finally arriving at an acceptable formula in the fifth century CE for belief in God the Father, God the Son and God the Holy Spirit.

However, where the Celts did have problems of belief was in their doctrine of mankind's relationship to God. They had a positive view of human nature and believed men and women were responsible for their own actions and therefore finding their own salvation. The Druidic Triads affirm:

There are three things excellent among worldly affairs: hating folly,
loving virtue, and endeavouring constantly to learn.

This optimistic view of man's ability to work out his own destiny and to achieve a harmonious relationship with God came into conflict with the more pessimistic teachings of the leaders of the Roman Church, and in particular St Augustine of Hippo in North Africa. The Celtic scholar, a monk called Pelagius, who became the focus of the dispute with St Augustine probably came from Wales and lived from about 360 to 430 CE. He was well-educated and of noble birth, though unfortunately most of what we know about him comes from his adversaries, as he was declared to be a heretic by the Roman Church.

In 429 CE St Germanus of Auxerre, who had been educated as a lawyer in Rome, was sent from Gaul on the first of his visits to Britain to counter the Pelagian heresy. His name is remembered in north Cornwall at the priory church of St Germans and in several other places in Britain where there are churches dedicated to him; his feast day is 31 July.

It took twenty years or more to master the full spectrum of Druidic knowledge and education was also of paramount importance to the Christian Celts. Certain monasteries became great centres of learning and repositories of knowledge. Schools were set up to educate young boys for the priesthood, and people like St Illtyd and St Ita of Killeedy, who reputedly educated St Brendan, were renowned for their wisdom and teaching.

In St Illtyd we have a man who, like St Martin before him, was a soldier. There are several stories of how he came to accept the Christian faith. One version tells that some of his troops fell into a swamp and were drowned. Illtyd himself very nearly lost his life too and this salutary brush with death was the supposed catalyst for his conversion.

Another tale relates how he came with his virtuous wife, Trynihid, to Glamorgan to serve under his cousin King Arthur. Here he met St Cadog, relinquished his military career, parted from his wife and chose to live as a monk, praying, fasting and distributing alms to the poor. One of the Welsh Triads says that he, along with St Cadog and Peredur, was one of the "three knights of the Court of Arthur who kept the Holy Grail".

Illtyd settled in the Vale of Glamorgan at Llanilltud Fawr, known as Llantwit Major in English. Trynihid, meanwhile, withdrew to a solitary place in the mountains and founded an oratory there. Her name is commemorated in Llantrihyd in Glamorgan, Llanrhidian on the Gower peninsula and Llandridian near St David's in Pembrokeshire.

Initially St Illtyd lived alone as a hermit, and the familiar anecdote of a hunted animal taking refuge in his cell is linked with him. It was a stag who fled to his sanctuary while the hunting dogs stayed outside barking. The creature became tame and Illtyd employed it to pull wagons loaded with timber to help build his monastery. The saint was known for his scholarship, piety and wisdom and many men were drawn to share in his life of prayer and service, and so the community at Llantwit Major flourished.

A large church comprising two parts, one each side of the central tower, now stands on the site of St Illtyd's original fifth-century monastery and college. The east church was built in the thirteenth century but the older west church, built by the Normans, is where the Celtic church would have been. This part of the building houses an important collection of Celtic stones and memorials. The headless shaft of the Cross of St Illtyd, also called the Samson Cross, has surfaces highly decorated with knotwork and key patterns. There are two inscriptions in Latin, one saying, "Samson placed this cross for his soul"; the name "Iltut" can be clearly seen on the reverse. The very tall Pillar of Samson stands nearby, again bearing a Latin inscription which mentions two eighth-century kings thought to have been buried here. Like Iona in Scotland, Llantwit Major was a royal burial-place.

The most complete monument is the Houelt Cross, the wheel-head and shaft of which are carved from one piece of stone. It is engraved in half-uncial script with the message, "In the name of God the Father and of the Son and of the Holy Spirit, Houelt prepared this cross for the soul of Res his father."

A window in the east church, dating from 1905, shows the saints associated with Llantwit Major: David, Patrick, Samson and of course Illtyd, who appears with a plough because throughout Wales he was celebrated for introducing an improved method of ploughing. At Llantwit Major, as their land was so low-lying, it regularly flooded when the river level rose and the sea encroached. A dyke was built to protect the monastery fields but it was breached on three occasions. They wrestled with the problem and eventually Illtyd decided that the community should leave the site and move further inland. However, that night he had a dream in which an angelic messenger forbade him to do so and gave him alternative instructions.

He was told to go to the shore the following day with his staff and hold it out against the rising waters. He did as he had been commanded and, as he advanced, the tide retreated; when he struck the ground with his staff a spring welled up on the spot. He knelt and prayed, giving thanks for the miracle and asking that the present shoreline should be the boundary of the sea.

There is some contention over Illtyd's place of birth. Some say he was a native of Armorica and thus Breton, and his cult is certainly widespread in Brittany. There are dedications to him centred on Léon, Vannes and Tréguier, but these may have come about when he sailed there with some ships bearing grain and seed-corn to relieve a famine. Others consider him to be a Welshman who was born near Brecon in 425 CE. About 4 miles east of Brecon there is a dedication to Illtyd at Llanhamlach, where he is supposed to have had a place

of seclusion. In a twelfth-century manuscript Gerald of Wales recalls how an unusual beast used to bring food and supplies to him here. The creature, resulting from the union of a horse and a stag, was wonderfully swift.

Despite his name meaning "one who is safe from all evil", Illtyd suffered persecution from two of the stewards of King Meirchion, who resented his community having land and not paying taxes. To avoid them he would withdraw to a cave by the River Ewenny, leaving St Samson in charge of the monastery. He also used to retreat there for times of solitude and prayer.

On one occasion he stayed in the cave for as long as one year and three days and nights. People were grieved at his disappearance from among them, for it was a very secret place. One day a messenger passed the mouth of the cave bearing a bell as a gift from St Gildas to St David. At the sound of the bell Illtyd emerged, asked him where he was going and rang the bell himself. The envoy continued on his way, but when the bell was duly given to David it remained silent. St David realized that Illtyd had held the bell and that he would like to keep it, so he sent it back to the saint as a token of affection. The messenger told the entire story to all the monks on his return to the monastery and Illtyd was fetched out of his solitude by them and reinstated as their guardian with much rejoicing.

As Illtyd lay dying, two abbots, Isanus and Atoclius, attended him. He welcomed them and, using his gift of seership, told them of their own impending deaths. He predicted his own departure from this world about midnight and said that Isanus would witness his soul rising like an eagle with golden wings. Isanus was also to see the soul of Atoclius rising like an eagle, but with leaden wings because he had loved the things of this world. Illtyd also told him that forty days later Isanus himself would die. Due to this timely warning, the soul of Atoclius was purified by the intercessory prayers of Isanus.

During his life Illtyd spent time at a community founded by St John Cassian near Marseilles and was also a disciple of St Germanus of Auxerre, who ordained him about 447 CE. In the Life of another Celtic saint, Samson of Dol, Illtyd is described as the most learned man among the Britons, being well-versed in both the Old and the New Testaments, and in every branch of philosophy, poetry and rhetoric, grammar and arithmetic.

Llantwit Major grew as a centre of educational excellence and many monks from the south of Ireland would have been educated there. Also numbered among its pupils were the saints Samson of Dol, Gildas de Rhuys, Paul Aurelian, also known as St Pol de Léon, who were all greatly honoured in Brittany, and possibly even St David himself.

In the fifth and sixth centuries CE there was a migration of Celtic Christians from south-west Britain and Wales to Brittany, then called Armorica. These refugees, fleeing from the pagan Saxons, took with them their customs and Christian faith, and in their new surroundings would have readily identified with the local culture and found much that was familiar. Even the language would not have been too strange, because these Celtic tongues share common

roots. Today the Breton language is still closely related to both Cornish and Welsh. Many Breton and Cornish place-names are prefixed by the syllable "*lan*", in the same way that many Welsh place names begin with "*llan*", meaning "enclosure". This usually marks the place where a Christian hermit or small groups of monks settled and built cells and an oratory.

Perhaps the most famous monastery in Brittany today that has Celtic links is at Landévennec near Brest, on the southern bank of the River Aulne. The name Landévennec comes from Lan-to-win-oc, meaning the "enclosure of Winwaloe", and was founded in 485 CE by St Winwaloe. Although born near St Brieuc, he was of Cornish descent, his parents having been part of the exodus in the fifth century. Initially he and his monks attempted to live on the nearby island of Tibidy, but it proved too difficult. He was given land for his enclosure by the local ruler, King Gradlon, whose grave can still be seen in the grounds of the monastery.

Little is known of the early history of Landévennec except that St Guénolé, the Breton name for Winwaloe, was its founder and first abbot. The monks kept his rule until 818 CE, when the rule of St Benedict, which is still adhered to today, was adopted. In common with many Celtic monasteries, it has had a violent history. In 913 CE it was burnt and sacked by the Vikings and the monks took their records and relics to Montreuil-sur-Mer in Picardy, where they founded another monastery. When it was safe, after an interval of thirty years or so, they returned to Landévennec to rebuild their old monastery. The community experienced both expansion and decline over the next 800 years and by the time of the French Revolution in 1789, there were only four monks at Landévennec. As a result the site was sold and the buildings fell into ruin.

However, the spirit of St Guénolé refused to die and in 1950 a plan to rebuild the monastery was announced. Eight years later work on the building was inaugurated, with a new abbey church being consecrated in 1965. Thousands of visitors made the journey to Landévennec in 1985 to celebrate the anniversary of the founding of the original monastery 1,500 years earlier, and each year there is a constant stream of pilgrims to visit this living Christian community which is still inspired by the traditions of the Breton saints and culture. It retains close links with Cornish Christians today through the Companions of St Guénolé, who make regular pilgrimages there.

Offering hospitality was an important feature of Celtic society and this practice was continued by the monastic communities. Here travellers and pilgrims could find shelter and sustenance. No one was turned from the door, as it was thought that an angel or even Jesus himself might be "entertained unawares". St Cuthbert's experience illustrates this. In Ripon one snowy day he attended to a passing visitor by washing his travel-stained feet and offering him food. When he returned from the kitchen, after a short absence to fetch some newly baked bread, he found the guest parlour empty. There were no footprints in the snow outside but lying on the table were three warm loaves, a gift from his heavenly guest.

*Left:*
Detail from the Gospel
of St Matthew,
Landévennec, Brittany.

*Left:*
Cross shaft in St Illtyd's
Church, Llantwit Major,
South Glamorgan.

*Right:*
St Illtyd's Church, Caldey
Island.

*Trim the cruisie's failing light,*
*the Son of God shall pass tonight,*
*shall pass at midnight dreary*
*the Son of Mary weary.*

*Lift the sneck and wooden bar*
*and leave the stranger's door ajar,*
*lest He may tarry lowly*
*the Son of Mary Holy.*

*Sweep the hearth and pile the peat*
*and set the board with bread and meat,*
*the Son of God may take it,*
*the Son of Mary brake it.*

Murdoch Maclean

The monasteries of Illtyd at Llantwit Major and Winwaloe at Landévennec were places of Christian learning and hospitality, replacing earlier Roman and Druidic centres of study in the Dark Ages. The Celtic monks were often concerned with improving the living standards of the lay people in the locality too. They introduced improved farming methods and tried to encourage the populace by their examples of good stewardship and husbandry. These practical skills fostered by the monks were balanced during the day by periods of prayer and education in the Christian faith. The monastic communities enabled men and women to use their God-given skills and gifts for the benefit not only of their own fellows, but that of visitors, travellers and the local community. With the collapse of the Roman administration in the fifth century CE, the monasteries increasingly filled an important vacuum and created opportunities for people to work together, sharing individual talents in a co-operative and constructive way.

Christian communities today have a similar role in helping people to discover their true selves, not only in a spiritual context but also by finding specific ways of using their abilities in the service of God and their neighbours. Most monasteries and religious houses receive guests, either individually or in groups, for a period of a day or a weekend, or for longer. Such visits may occur at a turning point in one's life, when a new sense of purpose and direction is being sought, or may be taken on a regular basis for quiet and reflection. The hospitality at such times is warm and friendly without being intrusive, the food simple and wholesome, and the atmosphere ordered and peaceful. There is usually a well-stocked library for private study. Sometimes silence is observed at certain times of the day and in particular parts of the building or grounds. Regular worship takes place in the chapel, though there is usually no pressure on the visitor to participate. Guests usually help by doing simple tasks, such as washing up after meals.

*I saw a stranger yestreen,*
*I put food in the eating place,*
*Drink in the drinking place,*
*Music in the listening place,*
*And in the sacred name of the Triune*
*He blessed myself and my house,*
*My cattle and my dear ones,*
*And the lark said in her song*
*Often, often, often*
*Goes the Christ in the stranger's guise.*

from *The Book of Cerne*

The larger the monastic community, the more diverse and numerous the tasks become: maintenance and repairs, cooking, gardening, receiving guests and visitors, administration and finance, staffing the bookshop or organizing the worship in the chapel. Each community is a microcosm of the wider world and shows that in following God's purposes we can use our experience, skills and resources for the common good.

*Be joyful brothers and sisters,*
*Keep your faith and do the little things*
*You have seen and heard with me.*

according to Gerald of Wales, this is
the last message of St David

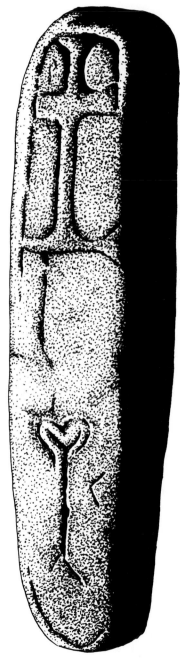

Cross-decorated
stone at
Castledermot,
County Kildare.

# A·U·G·U·S·T

*God to enfold me,*
  *God to surround me,*
*God in my speaking,*
  *God in my thinking.*

*God in my sleeping,*
  *God in my waking,*
*God in my watching,*
  *God in my hoping.*

*God in my life,*
  *God in my lips,*
*God in my soul,*
  *God in my heart.*

*God in my sufficing,*
  *God in my slumber,*
*God in mine ever-living soul,*
  *God in mine eternity.*

from the *Carmina Gadelica* (iii, 53)

THE FINAL major fire festival of the cycle, Lughnasad, is primarily a celebration of the grain harvest, when the first corn was cut at the time of the waning moon, and the first loaf was baked from it and then offered to the Goddess in thanksgiving. It marks the end of the summer and is a season of abundance and fruitfulness. The feast was associated with the Celtic god Lugh, who in Celtic art and mythology had golden armour and a magical shield; he is the sun king and the corn king who dies, or is harvested, at this time of the year. The forces which began to emerge at Imbolc in February are now starting to return to the earth. Like the other Celtic festivals, dates were not exact and Lughnasad would have lasted for many days either side of 1 August.

Lughnasad was taken over by the Church and replaced by Lammas or Loafmas, a celebration of harvest. In Scotland when the first corn was about to be cut the entire household, dressed in their finest clothes, would go to the harvest field to be present at such a significant moment. The head of the family, bareheaded and facing the sun, would cut a handful of corn with a sickle and, passing it three times round his head sunwise, would begin to sing. Then all would join in a hymn to the Lord of the harvest.

> *God, bless Thou Thyself my reaping,*
> *Each ridge, and plain, and field,*
> *Each sickle curved, shapely, hard,*
> *Each ear and handful in the sheaf,*
> > *Each ear and handful in the sheaf.*
>
> from the *Carmina Gadelica* (i,247)

On the feast day of the Virgin Mary, 15 August, a special Lammas bannock was baked, another pagan custom adopted by the Celtic Christians. The ritual is explained in the following incantation, which was sung as the head of the household, followed by his family, circled sunwise around the fire after consuming their pieces of bannock.

> *On the feast day of Mary the fragrant,*
> *Mother of the Shepherd of the flocks,*
> *I cut me a handful of the new corn,*
> *I dried it gently in the sun,*
> *I rubbed it sharply from the husk,*
> > *With mine own palms.*
>
> *I ground it in a quern of Friday,*
> *I baked it on a fan of sheep-skin,*
> *I toasted it to a fire of rowan,*
> *And I shared it round my people.*
>
> from *Carmina Gadelica* (i,195)

A ceremony called "Crying the Neck" is re-enacted by members of the Old Cornwall Society each year, the "neck" being the last remaining stalks of wheat in the field. The neck is cut and held aloft with triumphant cries, and then taken as a thanks-offering to the local church or chapel. Here we have a vestige of the pre-Christian Celtic belief in a triple goddess in her three guises as maiden,

mother and hag. The corn mother is slain and the last sheaf can either represent her continuing life as a young maid, or old age and death in her form as crone. The last stalks are often plaited into a figure or symbolic design and the resulting corn dolly kept in a suitable place until the next harvest.

It was R. S. Hawker, the nineteenth-century Cornish cleric, who in-augurated the present-day form of the harvest festival within the churches. He loved the natural world and used to scatter the floor of his church with herbs, such as wormwood, wild thyme and sweet marjoram, throughout the year. Like the Celtic saints before him, Hawker had a close affinity with God's creatures. Apparently birds used to flutter around him for food, and in one of his letters he tells how two mice were playing on his desk while he wrote.

When he left the vicarage to conduct services, he was often accompanied by his favourite dog and several cats which would follow him into the chancel. It was the habit of the dog to sit on the altar step behind his master while he conducted the service. When challenged about this, the cleric was adamant and replied, "Turn the dog out of the ark! All animals, clean and unclean, should find there a refuge."

To celebrate Lughnasad, fires were lit on primal mounds such as Silbury Hill in Wiltshire, and in late July and early August there were communal gatherings on many hills and mountains. Games were played, trials of strength undertaken, and dancing, singing and feasting were all enjoyed around the fires. On the Isle of Man great gatherings, called "Laa Lunys", took place at South Barrule and St Maughold's Head. Originally all these festivities would have had a religious purpose related to the sun and the harvest, and gradually some of these secular gatherings took on a sacred aspect once more and became Christian pilgrimages.

Every year, on the last Sunday of July, Christian pilgrims gather at Croagh Patrick, a dramatic, conical hill in County Mayo on the west coast of Ireland. It rises abruptly to a height of 2,500 feet from a mountain ridge on the southern shore of Clew Bay and has magnificent views over the sea and myriads of little islands. Although it is possible to visit and climb Croagh Patrick at any time of the year, this favourite date towards the end of July, sometimes known as Garland Sunday, is significant because of its proximity to the old pagan festival of Lughnasad.

Although there is no direct evidence that St Patrick visited this mountain, it would be surprising if he had not come to such a distinctive holy place during his thirty-year mission in Ireland. He is supposed to have spent the forty days and forty nights prior to Easter, the traditional Lenten season for Christian abstinence and penance, on the mountain in prayer and fasting, interceding for the Irish nation. Later traditions add vivid details to St Patrick's vigil on Croagh Patrick, telling how he was tormented by demons who appeared to him as black birds. Patrick responded by singing psalms, ringing his bell and then throwing it at them, causing them to flee.

In the Middle Ages Christian pilgrims also used to fast and pray on

Croagh Patrick during the forty days of Lent, in imitation of St Patrick, or if that proved too demanding, they would climb the mountain on 17 March, his feast day and the anniversary of his death. However, the modern focus is on the last Sunday of July, perhaps because of the persistent remembrance of the festival of Lughnasad over the years, or because of more practical considerations such as the better weather conditions and longer days during the summer.

There is a small oratory on the top of Croagh Patrick which fell into ruins over the centuries, but it was rebuilt and dedicated on 30 July 1905. Access to the mountain can be gained along rough tracks from either the eastern side or the western side. Most pilgrims approach from the east, starting their journey in the dark, so that they can reach the summit at dawn. There are three penitential stations on the mountain, one just before the place where the path is replaced by rocks and stones, and two more at the top. Most people who make the ascent have fasted since the previous day and some pilgrims climb the mountain barefoot, though this practice does not appear to be as popular as it once was. Either way, the terrain is hard on both shoes and feet. Masses are said on the mountain and people receive the sacrament before beginning their descent.

Another date connected with the harvest is St Bartholomew's Day, 24 August, when the setting sun appears to roll down the side of Croagh Patrick as you look from St Patrick's Chair, a large carved stone situated on the pilgrimage route from Ballintubber Abbey. For the pre-Christian Celts of St Patrick's time, this dramatic display would confirm the link between the sacred mountain and sun-worship. This ties in with the custom at midsummer and midwinter of rolling a wooden wheel, with straw twisted around it and set alight, down the side of a hill so that it resembled the sun revolving. Formerly Mount Brandon in County Kerry, Church Mountain in County Wicklow and Slieve Donard in County Down also had pilgrimages at this time, but now only the Croagh Patrick one survives.

Patrick's mission to Ireland in the fifth century involved conflict with many traditional Celtic beliefs and practices, and these would have included worship of the sun and the god Lugh, and the celebrations at the time of the festival of Lughnasad. Towards the end of his "Confession", which all scholars agree is the work of St Patrick himself, the author contrasts the sun-worship of the pagans with the worship of the true God:

> For the sun which we see rises day by day on our account, but it will
> never reign nor will its splendour last. Furthermore all those
> wretched men who worship it will come bitterly to punishment but
> we, on the other hand, who believe and worship Christ the true sun,
> who will never perish, nor will anyone who does his will, but will last
> into eternity as Christ also lasts into eternity, who reigns with God
> the omnipotent Father, and with the Holy Spirit before this age
> began, and now through all the ages of the ages.   Amen.

There are many sites associated with St Patrick both in Ireland and further afield. Near St Davids in Wales there is a ruined chapel at Whitesands Bay, and at Heysham, high above Morecambe Bay in Lancashire, the ruins of another small stone chapel, possibly dating from the ninth century, are both dedicated to the saint. Pilgrims to Glastonbury can visit St Patrick's Chapel in the abbey grounds. St Patrick himself travelled widely in Britain and on the continent of Europe, but it was in Ireland that he carried out his life's work and where he left his mark on the landscape of the country and the culture of the people.

At the age of sixteen, St Patrick was taken from his home somewhere on the west coast of Britain by Irish raiders. Various locations between the Severn estuary and the River Clyde have been suggested for his birthplace. He does not say exactly where he spent his years of captivity in Ireland and there are very few clues in his two extant writings, the "Confession" and the "Letter to the Soldiers of Coroticus". If he was taken to Ulster, and tradition favours County Antrim and the region around Mount Slemish, then the nearest area of Roman-occupied Britain where he might have lived would be just south of Hadrian's Wall in Cumbria. His abduction took place early in the fifth century CE, at the time when the Roman legions were preparing to withdraw from Britain, and they may already have left this most northerly part of the Roman Empire, thus encouraging the Irish to carry out their piratical raid.

During his six years of slavery, St Patrick spent many solitary hours as a shepherd in the forests and on the hills; in his loneliness he discovered God. He regretted not having paid attention to his lessons as a child, but may have remembered things told to him by his father, Calpurnius, who was a deacon, and his grandfather Potitus, who was a priest. He says he prayed up to 100 prayers day and night in the forests and the mountains, in all weather conditions.

> *Christ be with me, Christ within me,*
> *Christ behind me, Christ before me,*
> *Christ beside me, Christ to win me,*
> *Christ to comfort and restore me,*
> *Christ beneath me, Christ above me,*
> *Christ in quiet, Christ in danger,*
> *Christ in hearts of all that love me,*
> *Christ in mouth of friend and stranger.*
>
> from "St Patrick's Breastplate", translated by
> C. F. Alexander (1818–95)

Later, through the inspiration of a vision in which he saw a man, his soul-friend Victor, he returned to Ireland, but as bishop rather than slave. In the dream Victor brought letters to him from Ireland, one of which was called "The Voice of the Irish". When Patrick started to read the letter, he seemed to hear the voice of people who lived beside the Wood of Voclut, which is near the

western sea, begging him to come and walk among them again. We cannot know for certain where the Wood of Voclut is located, but the "western sea" is either the Irish Sea or the Atlantic Ocean. As Patrick began his missionary work in Ulster at Saul near Strangford Lough and then later in Armagh, this is further evidence that his place of captivity as a youth had indeed been in Ulster, but if the "western sea" is the Atlantic Ocean then his association with Croagh Patrick becomes much stronger.

The theme of exile is a familiar one among the Celtic saints and St Patrick never lost his consciousness of being a Romano-British citizen. Like St Paul in the New Testament, he was prepared to sacrifice his entitlements and his inheritance for the sake of the Christian faith. St Paul was able to boast about being a pure-blooded Jew, descended from the tribe which gave Israel its first king, and a strict Pharisee who kept the law in all its detail, yet he counted these privileges, as he saw them, as nothing in comparison with knowing Jesus Christ.

St Patrick also sold his birthright as a privileged and comfortable Roman citizen and, although he longed to return to his family and home in Britain and also to meet some of his Christian friends in Gaul, he was "bound in the Spirit not to see any of his relations" and did not want to risk the collapse of his work in Ireland by his absence. On a practical level, he probably sold his birthright to enable him to finance his Irish mission and to purchase some cows, the unit of currency in Ireland at the time.

Again, like St Paul, Patrick also suffered persecution and hardship, being seized and bound in chains. On another occasion some new Christians, recently baptized by Patrick and still in their white clothing with the oil shining on their foreheads, were butchered or captured by the soldiers of Coroticus and taken into slavery. It was this atrocity that prompted his angry letter to the British chieftain.

Yet the overriding impression gained from St Patrick's writings is not so much his concern with the physical danger he risked, but more the spiritual conflict he experienced; it was the dangers to the soul that exercised his efforts and energy. His lack of education, interrupted when he was sixteen, weighed heavily on his mind, but his spiritual condition was far more important to him. In the convention of the day, he writes of himself as a sinner and imperfect in many ways, but wants his readers to know that, despite all his faults and failings, the success of his Irish mission is based not on his own endeavours but entirely on God.

Station Island in Lough Derg, County Donegal, along with Croagh Patrick, is one of the oldest places of pilgrimage in Ireland. It attracts thousands of pilgrims each year to endure its rigours. The historical link with St Patrick dates only from the twelfth century, and it may be that an earlier pilgrimage was superseded when the Augustinian monks who established a monastery here decided that St Patrick would be a greater magnet for pilgrims than the local and relatively unknown St Dabeoc, who is still the patron of the place. He was

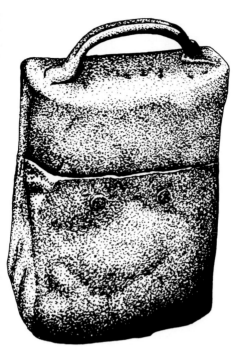

St Patrick's Bell.

the son of a Welsh prince and a noble British woman called Marcella, and in the Welsh Triads his family is described as being one of the "three holy families of Wales". One night, while he and his monks were keeping a vigil, they saw a powerful, brilliant light coming from the north. Staring in wonder, they turned to their master Dabeoc and he interpreted the sign as foretelling the birth and life of St Columba. The ruins of the medieval church on nearby Saint's Island are believed to be on the site of Dabeoc's original foundation.

Station Island derives its name from the penitential exercises called "stations" which modern pilgrims observe here. There is a set pattern which they are expected to follow for three days and nights without sleep. Barefoot and on a ration of only dry bread and black tea, they pray continually while making a round of the stones known as "Saint's beds", either standing, kneeling or walking as they pray. An all-night vigil takes place inside the basilica on the tiny island concluding with Mass at dawn.

Also on Station Island is St Patrick's Purgatory, a cave in which pilgrims during the Middle Ages used to be locked for twenty-four hours after spending fifteen days in preparation by prayer and fasting. The site owes much of its fame to a twelfth-century account by Henry of Saltray of how a knight called Owen spent fifteen days in penance at Lough Derg before embarking on one of the Crusades to Palestine. Owen's vivid experiences and visions led to the development of the Roman Catholic doctrine of Purgatory and inspired many writers, including Dante, the author of *The Divine Comedy*.

Although topographically different, Lough Derg is similar to Croagh Patrick in that the large lake lies in empty countryside in a remote part of Ireland, 4 miles from the nearest village. Because of its isolation and austerity, it has escaped much of the commercialization of other pilgrimage sites, despite the large numbers who come each summer.

What the two main Patrick sites have in common is an emphasis on penitence, prayer and fasting. These are not common or popular practices today, but they are aids to self-discovery and spiritual growth. Surprisingly, following the spiritual path means becoming simpler and simpler, as the truths sink deeper into our lives, and this is the same for all religious traditions. The process of stripping away the material comforts of everyday life helps us to sharpen our perceptions and to explore new dimensions. Fasting and silence remove us from the ordinary, so that the spirit is liberated and enabled to embrace true values. After the rigours of climbing Croagh Patrick or spending three days fasting and praying at Lough Derg, the pilgrim's soul is cleansed and purified, thus awakening it to the eternal nature of life and to its potential. The harvest of the soul takes on a new dimension in this context and brings to mind the fact that man does not live by bread alone.

*Jesu, give me forgiveness of sins,*
*Jesu, keep my guilt in my memory,*
*Jesu, give me the grace of repentance,*
*Jesu, give me the grace of forgiveness,*
*Jesu, give me the grace of submission,*
*Jesu, give me the grace of earnestness,*
*Jesu, give me the grace of lowliness,*
*To make a free confession at this time . . .*

*. . . Jesu, take pity upon me,*
   *Jesu, have mercy upon me,*
   *Jesu, take me to Thee,*
   *Jesu, aid my soul.*

*A cause of grief is sin,*
   *A cause of anguish is death,*
*A cause of joy is repentance*
   *And cleansing in the river of health.*

from the *Carmina Gadelica* (iii, 257)

Another ancient prayer associated with St Patrick, although not written by him, is the eighth-century protective incantation called "St Patrick's Breastplate". These charms were widespread and there is a whole series of breastplate prayers or *loricae* in the Celtic oral tradition.

*I bind unto myself today*
*The strong name of the Trinity,*
*By invocation of the same,*
*The Three in One and One in Three,*
*Of whom all nature hath creation;*
*Eternal Father, Spirit, Word:*
*Praise to the lord of my salvation,*
*Salvation is of Christ the Lord.*

from "St Patrick's Breastplate", translated by C. F. Alexander (1818–95)

Not only are these prayers of protection but they teach us how to prepare for daily life, how to put on "the mind of Christ". Our potential as Christian pilgrims is to become more Christ-like as we perceive the Christ in others and thus contribute towards bringing the Kingdom of Heaven here on earth.

# S·E·P·T·E·M·B·E·R

*O Michael of the angels*
*And the righteous in heaven,*
*Shield thou my soul*
   *With the shade of thy wing;*
*Shield thou my soul*
   *On earth and in heaven;*

*From foes upon earth,*
*From foes beneath earth,*
*From foes in concealment*
*Protect and encircle*
   *My soul 'neath thy wing,*
    *Oh my soul with the shade of thy wing!*

from the *Carmina Gadelica* (iii, 149)

DURING THE SPRING, on 23 April, those people who live in England celebrate the feast of St George, their patron saint. His day falls at a time of expansion in the seasonal cycle, between the spring equinox and the summer solstice. Trees and plants are coming into leaf and the daylight is lengthening. He is very much a saint of the earth and of outward things.

At the autumn equinox in September, the sun moves into the zodiacal sign of Libra the scales; day and night are balanced and of equal length once more. It is a time when the earth energies, and our own, start to retreat and go down into the roots.

The Celt, for whom the spiritual world was and is a powerful reality, has a

strong devotion to St George's heavenly counterpart, the archangel St Michael. They are like two sides of the same coin: St George pointing the way on the outward journey, balanced by St Michael, who aids us on the inner spiritual one. His feast falls on 29 September, between the autumn equinox and the winter solstice, when the earth is withdrawing into itself in preparation for the winter. Thus he encourages us to go within and to explore the inner realms of our soul's journey.

These two saints are the guardians of the dragon currents, those earth energies that run through the land. They have control over these natural forces which, when channelled and directed, bring healing and prosperity to the land. It is fitting that Michaelmas falls at the time of the year when many people in the northern hemisphere are celebrating their harvest festivals and giving thanks for the bounty of the earth and gifts of creation. It is the fulfilment of the feast of St George at the time of the spring planting.

St Michael also has jurisdiction over those inner energies that we encounter on our inward journey. He is known as a dragon-slaying saint and is often portrayed in conquering stance, holding a lance which is piercing a great serpent through the head or throat. Through the ages this has been seen by the Christian Church as the victory of good over evil, the destruction of sin, and the triumph of morality and virtue. Where Michael is mentioned in the Bible he is depicted as captain of the heavenly hosts and vanquisher of dark forces.

However, without darkness there can be no light. This concept is beautifully shown in the Taoist yin–yang symbol, where the black and white are equal and shaped to fit into each other; they are perfectly in balance. Like the autumn equinox, St Michael's feast falls within the astrological sign of Libra, the scales, a symbol of balance and harmony.

Could it be that St Michael's lance, as shown on the cover of the Chalice Well at Glastonbury, is the point that holds in balance the forces of light and dark? He tames the dragon and subdues the energy rather than killing it. In a similar way we are faced with coming to terms with our inner darknesses and learning to balance those things within us that hinder the growth of the human soul. In this present age of brutality and violence, perhaps we need to befriend our dragon rather than destroy it, and in the process be gentle with ourselves.

> *Valiant Michael of the white steeds,*
> *Who subdued the Dragon of blood,*
> *For love of God, for pains of Mary's Son,*
> *Spread thy wing over us, shield us all,*
>    *Spread thy wing over us, shield us all.*
>
> from the *Carmina Gadelica* (i, 193)

The opposite astrological signs to Libra in the zodiac rule the head and throat. Rather than the body, this is where the dragon is usually pierced in depictions of the saint. The implications are that Michael helps us to subdue

and overcome the ego, the lesser self; then we can find balance and harmony in joining with our higher selves.

As might be expected, many of the churches on the Michael and Mary energy lines are dedicated to these saints, or St George. St Margaret of Antioch and St Catherine of Alexandria are also remembered as dragon-slayers, and dedications to them are in evidence on or near the dragon currents. The early Celtic saints often chose to settle close to these natural forces as well.

The village of St Buryan to the west of Penzance is sandwiched between the Michael Line and the Mary Line and was at one time a religious centre of some importance. The Irishwoman Buryan, daughter of a Munster chieftain, first settled here near Land's End in the fifth century CE. Around 930 CE King Athelstan rested here after a battle against the Danes. He took his Communion in the oratory and vowed that if he was successful in conquering the last Danish stronghold in the Isles of Scilly he would build a larger church. He triumphed over his enemies and kept his word, granting the privilege of sanctuary to St Buryan. He also established a college of canons in place of the old Celtic foundation where a body of priests lived, worked and studied together in a community. St Buryan's feast day in May is still marked by "Buryan Feast", which is not only the patronal festival of the parish church but a celebration for the whole community with services, sporting events and concerts. In Cornwall these "Feasts" embrace the sacred and the secular, and the saints concerned are often considered not to be the exclusive property of the church but to belong to all the local people. After St Buryan the two energy currents continue to St Michael's Mount, where they cross over each other.

Further north on the Mary Line in Cornwall, in the relative flatness of Goss Moor, is a dramatic rocky cliff called Roche Rock. Partly hollowed out of this rock is a hermitage and chapel dedicated to St Michael. The present structure was built in 1409 and is accessible only by climbing an iron ladder. St Conan, one of the first bishops of Cornwall, is said to have been resident here at one time, before he moved to St Michael's Mount, and he is the patron of the local parish church.

After leaving Cornwall, the next axial point of the two currents is at Brentor, on the edge of Dartmoor in Devon, where the church of St Michael stands on an elevated outcrop of volcanic rock, 1,100 feet above sea-level. The saint, holding a sword and a pair of scales, can be seen in a modern stained-glass window behind the altar at the east end of the church.

Crediton was the seat of the original bishopric of Devon and Cornwall before it was transferred to Exeter, and here St Boniface, who was of Anglo-Saxon stock, was born. He was murdered in 775 CE because of his missionary activities in Europe. The lines cross here and again at Creech St Michael Church in Somerset, and at Burrow Mump, an artificial mound surmounted by a ruined St Michael church. This small hill is made of red clay unknown in the immediate area, and forms the nose of the Girt Dog of Langport, the figure which guards the Glastonbury Zodiac to the south-west.

*Opposite:*
St Michael the
Archangel,
Glastonbury Tor,
Roche Rock and St
Michael's Mount,
Cornwall, dragon
carving from
Penmon Priory,
Anglesey, and the
Chalice Well at
Glastonbury.

At Glastonbury itself the energy currents cross in the abbey ruins, in the Chalice Well gardens, and on the side of the Tor, where they snake backwards and forwards around the contours of the hill. Again, a ruined church dedicated to St Michael dominates the summit.

In the parish church at Avebury in Wiltshire, which stands just outside the circle of stones, there is a font showing a human figure, possibly a bishop, with a spiked staff or crozier striking a dragon on the head. The serpent has the bishop's foot in his mouth, reminding us of the passage addressed to the serpent in the third chapter of Genesis concerning Eve's offspring: "He shall bruise your head, and you shall bruise his heel."

After leaving Avebury, the Michael Line and the Mary Line continue across England through Ogbourne St George, where the Celtic solar deity Og or Ock was superseded by the Christian saint and both are remembered in the name of the village. The lines cross at the Sinodun Hills near Dorchester-on-Thames, Royston Cave in Hertfordshire, and again at Bury St Edmunds, before finally reaching the ruined St Margaret's Church at Hopton-on-Sea in Norfolk.

The Celts had a particular devotion to St Michael and this has been retained: whereas St George has been adopted as the patron of England, the Cornish still regard Michael as their defender. The heavenly angels were a very real presence and were regarded as both guides and protectors, each person having their own guardian who could be asked for aid at any time.

*Thou angel of God who hast charge of me*
*From the dear Father of mercifulness,*
*The shepherding kind of the fold of the saints*
*To make round about me this night;*

*Drive from me every temptation and danger,*
*Surround me on the sea of unrighteousness,*
*And in the narrows, crooks, and straits,*
*Keep thou my coracle, keep it always.*

*Be thou a bright flame before me,*
*Be thou a guiding star above me,*
*Be thou a smooth path below me,*
*And be a kindly shepherd behind me,*
*To-day, to-night, and for ever.*

*I am tired and I a stranger,*
*Lead thou me to the land of angels;*
*For me it is time to go home*
*To the court of Christ, to the peace of heaven.*

from the *Carmina Gadelica* (i, 49)

St Michael is the patron saint of sea and boats, and there are three power sites connected with him that guard the western sea approaches to Britain, Ireland and the continent of Europe: Skellig Michael off the west coast of Ireland, St Michael's Mount in Cornwall and Mont St Michel in France.

Some 8 miles off the south-west coast of Ireland lie the remote Skelligs, three small islands, the largest of which is called Skellig Michael. It is an awe-inspiring place with its distinctive jagged shape and steep sides, and a challenge to any pilgrim. Access is usually by boat from Valentia Island in County Kerry, and if the swell of the sea does not deter the visitor, then the precipitous cliffs, combined with a 20-foot rise and fall in the tide, can be a daunting prospect. Skellig Michael is only $\frac{1}{2}$ mile long and $\frac{1}{4}$ mile wide, and rises to 715 feet at its highest point.

It is not certain when Christian monks first settled on this inaccessible rock. Because of the harshness of the terrain, the population was never large and the inhabitants probably lived as hermits rather than as an organized monastic community. The island was raided by the Vikings in the ninth century CE, though the monks continued to occupy the island until the twelfth century, when they moved to Ballinskelligs on the mainland.

The remains of monastic buildings cling to the rock on a small shelf 540 feet above the sea, at the top of a steep flight of stone steps. Part-way up this steep ascent there is a small green resting place known as Christ's Saddle. The path continues to a second plateau enclosed by a dry-stone wall or *cashel* where five stone beehive cells, similar in construction to the Gallarus Oratory on the Dingle peninsula, nestle in a tightly packed group. These windowless cells, or *clochans*, are massively constructed, with stone walls 6 feet thick. Beside them is a tiny oratory with a doorway and a window. A similar beehive cell can be seen in the monastic settlement of Inishmurray, 4 miles off the coast of County Sligo. Lower down there is a sixth *clochan*, another small oratory, two wells, various crosses and slabs, and the ruins of a medieval church dedicated to St Michael. The buildings have remained in such good condition due to the mild climate of this area and the lack of frost. Small fertile grassed areas called the Monks' Gardens are found on a series of terraces and it is thought that the monks brought the topsoil from the mainland.

> *Like mighty ships that sail Atlantic foam*
> *The Skellig Isles parade the Kerry coast*
> > *It's a strange place*
> > *With a needle's eye*
> > *Where shipwrecks lie*
>
> *Where the King of the World*
> *Rested for a while*
> *And a place for the pilgrim*
> *A sanctuary of time*

Beehive cells or *clochans* on Skellig Michael, County Kerry.

*Fourteen steps to nowhere*
*Out of solid stone*
*Don't lead us to the Heavens*
*Or lead us to the sea*

*The Vikings came to plunder and destroy*
*But to this day the holy relics stand*
    *In a blind man's cove*
    *Where the wailing woman sighs*
    *And the seagulls cry*

*A journey to these islands so rare*
*The sound of screaming souls that fill the air*
    *A thousand wings*
    *Against the sky*
    *And grey seals disguised*

    song by Ciaran Brennan of Clannad

There is some debate as to whether Mont St Michel is in Brittany or Normandy. It is in an estuary where three rivers converge and one of these, the Couesnon, is the border, causing some people to say the island is the property of Normandy when the tide is out and belongs to Brittany when surrounded by the sea. The sands are exposed at low water and it is possible to walk across from Genets on the northern side of the bay, though care needs to be taken because of quicksands and it is advisable to join an organized group with a guide. While Skellig Michael is remote, Mont St Michel is easily accessible, being linked to the mainland by a causeway 1 mile long to the south. It is a striking granite pinacle rising to 500 feet which is made to look even taller by the spire of the church on the summit. Much of the south of the island has been built on, giving it the feel of a village. The present Benedictine monastery dates from the eleventh to the thirteenth centuries, replacing an earlier foundation.

A legend relates how Bishop Aubert of Avranches received a visitation from the archangel Michael in 708 CE and was instructed to build a chapel which was to be dedicated to him. Apparently the bishop was rather reluctant to take the vision seriously, and the archangel had to prod him firmly on the head with a finger to make his point. The bishop's skull is on display in St Gervais' basilica and the resulting hole can be seen. Legend also tells us that St Michael fought a duel with the devil at nearby Mont Dol, an ancient mound which was an island at one time. The marks reputedly made by the adversary's claws as he fell and the print of the archangel's foot as he returned to his stronghold at Mont St Michel are visible.

The twelfth-century writer Geoffrey of Monmouth tells us that King Arthur, while on his way to a military campaign in Gaul, had a dream of a terrifying fight between a dragon and a flying bear. Arthur interpreted this dream to mean that he would soon find himself in mortal combat with a giant. He learned that a woman called Helena had been abducted by such an ogre and taken to Mont St Michel. After a vicious contest, Arthur slew the monster but was too late to save the captive from death.

Bishop Aubert sent messengers to Monte Gargano in Italy, where the archangel Michael had appeared. They returned with a piece of the red cloak that Michael had been wearing and a portion of the altar on which he had placed his foot.

The third site, St Michael's Mount, is set like a jewel in the curve of Mount's Bay in the far south-west of Cornwall. It has been identified with Ictis, mentioned in 25 CE by the Roman historian Diodorus Siculus as a place used for metal-trading with the continent of Europe and the Mediterranean. Here tin from Cornwall and gold and copper from Ireland changed hands, and Joseph of Arimathea may well have been familiar with the island.

In 495 CE some fishermen are said to have had a vision of the archangel Michael standing high above them on a western promontory, now known as Michael's Chair, or Cader Myghal in Cornish. According to the legend, he

"opened their eyes": that is, he awoke their inner vision. Consequently a chapel to this guardian of high places was built and it became an important place of pilgrimage.

As an act of faith, people used to climb out on to a second stone chair built by the monks as a lantern in the church tower. In the eleventh century Edward the Confessor established a priory on St Michael's Mount and granted authority over it to the abbey of Mont St Michel, its companion island in France. During the following century a Benedictine priory, which took nine years to complete, was established and it was again supervised by the French mother-house. Initially a prior and twelve monks formed the community, and new members who joined were expected to cross to France to receive a blessing from the abbot. It remained a monastery until 1425, when it was suppressed by Henry V, but it still continued as a place of pilgrimage for the faithful and was attributed with miraculous cures. Among its relics was the jawbone of St Apollonia of Alexandria, who, in the third century, had all her teeth broken by violent blows and was then burnt to death for refusing to recite blasphemies.

Pilgrims would make the crossing from Chapel Rock on the beach at Marazion, where a chapel dedicated to St Catherine stood until 1645, when it was destroyed during the Civil War. Each pilgrim would, as an act of penance, add one stone to the causeway.

A pilgrim cross used to stand half-way along the route and its stone socket is still visible. The granite Mount Cross that stands in the castle grounds is particularly interesting, as it has three crosses carved on its surface and also the smallest figure of Christ to be found on any of the Cornish Celtic crosses. There isn't a religious community on St Michael's Mount today, but the church there is used regularly for public worship throughout the summer months.

For the Scottish Gaels the feast in honour of St Michael was the highlight of the year, and here pagan and Christian customs overlapped considerably. On St Michael's Eve the men of the community spent the evening and night keeping guard over their horses, for it was permissible to "steal" them from neighbours on this night for "feast-riding" as long as they were returned unharmed. St Michael is also the patron saint of horses and they were used on St Michael's Day itself for a pilgrimage to the burial-ground of the ancestors and for racing later in the day. The women didn't retire to bed on Michaelmas Eve either, and instead they attended to a variety of household tasks. A male lamb without spot or blemish called the *uan Mìcheil*, or "Michael lamb", which represented the "fruits of the flocks", was killed. Also carrots were brought in. These would have been gathered during the afternoon on Carrot Sunday preceding Michaelmas and the small bunches tied with thread, usually red, and stored near the house ready for use. They were generally given by women to men as tokens of fertility and prosperity.

A cake called the *struan Mìcheil* was baked by the eldest daughter of the house under her mother's direction. It was made from all of the kinds of cereal

grown on the farm during the year and represented the "fruits of the field". The resulting flour was moistened with sheep's milk and baked on a lamb-skin. The cooking fire was made only from woods regarded as sacred, such as rowan and oak.

> *Each meal beneath my roof,*
> *They will all be mixed together,*
> *In the name of God the Son,*
> > *Who gave them growth.*
>
> *Milk, and eggs, and butter,*
> *The good produce of our own flock,*
> *There shall be no dearth in our land,*
> > *Nor in our dwelling.*
>
> *In the name of Michael of my love,*
> *Who bequeathed to us the power,*
> *With the blessing of the Lamb,*
> > *And of His Mother.*

from the *Carmina Gadelica* (i, 213)

As well as a large family *struan*, smaller ones were made for individuals even if they were away or had died. If they were absent, the cakes were kept carefully until their return; if they had died, the cakes were shared among the family and close friends of the departed person, or given to the poor. These little cakes were either triangular for the Holy Trinity, five-sided for the Trinity plus Mary and Joseph, seven-sided as symbolic of the seven mysteries, nine-sided for the nine archangels, or round, symbolizing eternity.

The people took the *struans* with them to church to be blessed when they went to Mass early on St Michael's Day. On their return, the cake and the cooked lamb were ceremonially cut into small pieces, placed in baskets and distributed to the poor of the district. The next event of the day was to go to the burial-ground and, after prayer and supplication, to circuit it sunwise, the people following behind the priest, and as many as possible mounted on horseback. After this came the sports, horse-racing and an evening dance where gifts and tokens were exchanged freely.

> *The compassing of the saints be upon you,*
> *The compassing of the angels be upon you;*
> > *Oh the compassing of all the saints*
> > *And of the nine angels be upon you.*

from the *Carmina Gadelica* (iii, 205)

# O·C·T·O·B·E·R

*Since Thou Christ it was who didst buy the soul —*
*At the time of yielding the life,*
*At the time of pouring the sweat,*
*At the time of offering the clay,*
*At the time of shedding the blood,*
*At the time of balancing the beam,*
*At the time of severing the breath,*
*At the time of delivering the judgment,*
*Be its peace upon Thine own ingathering;*
*Jesus Christ Son of gentle Mary,*
*Be its peace upon Thine own ingathering,*
*        O Jesus! upon Thine own ingathering.*

*And may Michael white kindly,*
*High king of the holy angels,*
*Take possession of the beloved soul,*
*And shield it home to the Three of surpassing love,*
*        Oh! to the Three of surpassing love.*

from the *Carmina Gadelica* (i, 121)

*O*CTOBER is the final month of the Celtic year, when outside tasks need to be completed while there is still enough daylight, a time for gathering in what remains of the harvest and making preparations for the long winter ahead. It is natural that with the increasing hours of darkness the Celts should turn their thoughts to death and the afterlife, and much of Celtic culture was

concerned with the beliefs and rituals surrounding these matters. The new year festival of Samhain comes at the end of the month, when the ancestral spirits were honoured and drew close, reminding them that death is only a door from this world into the next. It is a liminal time when the boundaries between the worlds are not well defined and the spirits infuse this world of the senses, not that these two dimensions are ever far apart for the Celt.

They believed that the soul of a person lived on after physical death, not simply in a disembodied existence but continuing the life journey in a different dimension. The head was regarded as the seat of the soul or the centre of spiritual power, and consequently heads were often taken as trophies of war; it was thought that a warrior who died in battle was particularly blessed in the life after death.

Stories of islands to the west of the known world through the Pillars of Hercules, that is, the Straits of Gibraltar, were very familiar in Greek and Roman mythology. For the Celts, the Isles of the Blest, the Promised Land for the departed, also lay in the west towards the setting sun, and isolated islands off their coasts became identified with this idea. These islands were reached by crossing the waters of death, in much the same way as the ancient Greeks crossed the River Styx in their mythology, and many locations have been suggested, including Iona, Bardsey, Anglesey, the Aran Islands and the Isles of Scilly. They were places without disease, pain or decay: worlds of beauty and delight, with music and feasting, where it was perpetual summer. As with any mythological paradise, the approach to it was difficult and not without trial, but the arrival was always blessed with abundance.

Bardsey, a few miles off the Lleyn peninsula in north Wales, is known in Welsh as Ynys Enlli, "island in the currents", because of the strong seas which flow between it and the mainland. There is one tradition that it was the Celtic Isle of Avalon, where the fatally wounded King Arthur, accompanied by three queens, was taken in a barge to be healed after the battle of Camlan. Avalon means "island of apples" and is a title also applied to Glastonbury. The apple was a Celtic symbol of life and fertility and was sacred to the early British people, and thus Avalon becomes the equivalent of the Jewish Promised Land, a land of apples rather than of milk and honey. In the Irish story of *The Voyage of Bran*, the Otherworld goddess is symbolized by an apple branch.

The island became a favourite place of St Dyfrig, one of the earliest Welsh saints and a contemporary of St David. Like St Martin of Tours, he was a hermit and usually spent the season of Lent in meditation and solitude; he chose Ynys Pyr, now Caldey Island, off the coast of south Wales for this purpose, where there is a Roman Catholic community of monks today. Dyfrig was given the title "Papa", a term used by Celtic Christians for a revered teacher and missionary, and established his principal monastic settlement at Hentland, near Ross-on-Wye. Most of the churches dedicated to him are in the Wye valley and Herefordshire, where he is also remembered by the name St Devereux. After he became a bishop, he went as one of the leaders of the Celtic Church in Wales

Ruins of the abbey, Bardsey Island.

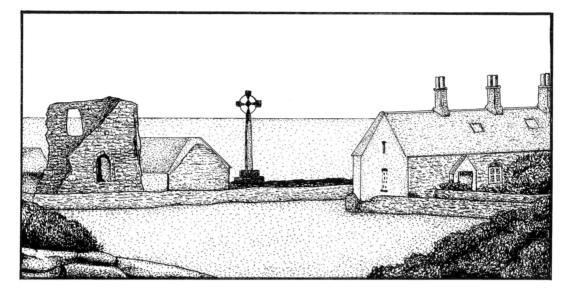

Puffin Island, also known as Priestholme or Ynys Seiriol.

to the Synod of Brevi, which was called to denounce the heresy of Pelagianism and held at the place now called Llanddewi Brefi in Dyfed. His presence, along with that of St Deiniol, persuaded the reluctant St David to attend.

Later writers make Dyfrig an archbishop at the City of the Legions, thought by some to be Caerleon in south Wales, where the Romans had an important and strategic fort. Another theory suggests that the City of the Legions is Chester, near the present-day border with north Wales and close to the important Celtic monastery at Bangor Is-coed, on the River Dee. However, Dyfrig preferred to live as a hermit and so he resigned his episcopal position and retired with some of his companions to Bardsey, where he eventually died and was buried. About 600 years later in 1120, his remains were moved from Bardsey to Llandaff in south Wales, no doubt to help boost its claim to be the foremost diocese in all Wales.

The Celts suffered a disastrous defeat in about 605 CE when the Saxons conquered Chester and destroyed the monastery at nearby Bangor Is-coed. Over 1,000 monks perished and many of the survivors fled to Bardsey, where they joined the monastery which had been established by St Cadfan in the fifth century. Cadfan had migrated northwards, having originally come from Brittany, and on his way founded a church at Tywyn on the coast near Aberdovey, before settling on Bardsey and becoming the first abbot there. St Cadfan's church in Tywyn is known as the "mother of Bardsey" and contains the sixth-century Cadfan Stone inscribed in early Welsh.

Bardsey acquired a reputation as a place of great sanctity because of the many saints buried there, including St Dyfrig and St Deiniol. Tradition says that it became the last resting place for as many as 20,000 saints, although this is probably an exaggeration as the island is only 1½ miles long by ½ mile wide, and part of it is a steep hill, Mynydd Enlli, unsuitable for burials. According to a medieval writer, Bardsey was known as the "Rome of Britain" because of its remoteness, and three pilgrimages here were the equivalent of one pilgrimage to Rome.

> Me, the poet Meilyr, a pilgrim to Peter,
> The gate-ward who assesses qualities of perfection,
> When the time to rise will come for us
> All who are entombed, support Thou me.
> Awaiting the call, may I be in the precincts
> Of the monastery against which beats the tide,
> Which is secluded, and of undying fame,
> With its graveyard in the bosom of the sea,
> The Isle of wondrous Mary, holy isle of the saints
> Glorious within it resurrection to await
> Christ of the prophesied Cross, who knows me, will deliver me
> From a banished existence in violent hell;
> The Creator, who created me, will receive me
> Among the saintly parish of the band of Enlli.

> Meilyr Brydydd (early twelfth century),
> translated from the Welsh by J. Lloyd-Jones

Pilgrims embarked for Bardsey at Aberdaron and so the last resting place on the mainland was the village of Llangwnnadl, where the church used to contain the shrine of St Gwynhoedl. He lived during the sixth century and was reputed to be one of the sons of the Welsh chieftain Seithenyn; like his brothers, he was a member of the monastic community at Bangor Is-coed. His settlement was one of the earliest on the Lleyn peninsula, and in the south wall of the church there is a tombstone with a Celtic cross which was discovered when the present church buildings were being renovated in 1940. A Latin inscription on one of the pillars in the north arcade records the burial of

St Gwynhoedl, although there is a rival tombstone recording his burial at Llanbedrog on the south side of the peninsula.

In the Middle Ages, pilgrims who followed the route south sometimes went beyond Bardsey and continued by boat across Cardigan Bay to St Davids. Later, in the eighteenth century, similar journeys were undertaken by large numbers of people who walked from north Wales, down the Lleyn peninsula and then sailed southwards to the coast of Cardiganshire before continuing on foot to Llangeitho, to hear the Welsh revivalist preacher Daniel Rowlands.

The pilgrims' routes to Bardsey from both north and mid-Wales converge on the Lleyn peninsula at Clynnog Fawr, where St Beuno established a collegiate church in 616 CE, and then continue along the north coast, passing several pilgrims' churches on the way. The smallest of these is the attractive building at Pystill near Nevyn, where there is a round font with Celtic knotwork. It is also dedicated to St Beuno, the uncle of St Winefride of Holywell. He was well known as a healer and legend tells how he brought his niece back to life by restoring her severed head following the violent actions of Caradog, an unwelcome suitor. Many pilgrims through the ages would have visited this tiny hospice church and bathed their weary feet in a lotion made from the wild plant Lady's bedstraw, which still grows in the churchyard. A few miles to the south of the pilgrims' route on the Lleyn peninsula at Llangybi is Cybi's Well. This saint was the great-grandson of King Geraint of Cornwall and there are churches dedicated to him in that county at Tregony and Duloe, where he founded monasteries, as well as in Wales. After travelling through south Wales and spending four years on the Aran Islands in Ireland with St Enda, he settled on Anglesey with his companion St Seiriol.

A charming story relates how St Seiriol used to walk part-way each week to meet St Cybi, who had his cell on the opposite side of the island in the grounds of the abandoned Roman fort at Holyhead, still known in Welsh as Caer Gybi. Cybi walked eastwards towards the sun for the encounter with his fellow hermit at a place called Clorach, near Llanerchymedd, and so was nicknamed Cybi the Dark, as his skin became tanned, and Seiriol, who had his back to the sun as he walked, was known as Seiriol the Fair.

The island of Ynys Mon, or Anglesey in English, is rich in ancient sites. One of the earliest Celtic settlements was at Penmon near Beaumaris, where St Seiriol built his cell, the foundations of which can be seen adjacent to the holy well named after him. He is buried on nearby Puffin Island, also called Priestholme or Ynys Seiriol, a short distance from the south-eastern tip of Ynys Mon. Like Bardsey and Iona, this small limestone island was the burial-place of many saints and rulers, including St Seiriol's cousin, the sixth-century king Maelgwn Gwynedd, who established a priory at Penmon. Ynys Seiriol is now uninhabited and only the ruins of a twelfth-century church and monastic buildings remain.

In common with many monastic settlements, Penmon was raided by the Vikings and the priory was burnt in 971 CE. The present buildings date from the

twelfth century, and at the west end of the church there is a stone cross with a carving of St Antony of Egypt, which used to stand outside a short distance away but was moved inside to prevent further erosion by the weather.

It was not only the Celts in Wales who looked westwards to the Isles of the Blest. The Irish Celts also had their Promised Land across the sea in the direction of the setting sun and in pre-Christian times this Otherworld was called Tír na n'Óg, meaning the Land of the Eternally Young. The story of *The Voyage of St Brendan* begins with an account by the monk Barrind of his visit to the Promised Land of the Saints. When Brendan and his companions eventually reached the same destination, they were bathed in a brilliant light and before them they could see an open country covered in apple trees laden with ripe fruit. The monks ate as much as they could and drank from the springs of pure water. The island was more than forty days' walk in length and had a wide river flowing through the middle of it. There was an abundance of precious stones and perpetual light throughout the year. A young man welcomed Brendan and his companions and told them that this was the place they had been seeking for so long. He instructed Brendan to fill his ship with all the good things from the land and then to return to his own country, because the day of his death was approaching. This Brendan did and, after putting his affairs in order, gave up his spirit and died in the arms of his disciples.

St Enda, who trained in the monastery of Candida Casa, Whithorn, is regarded as the father of Irish monasticism and his Rule was particularly strict. During the fifth century he lived on Inishmore, the largest of the three Aran Islands, and a small stone church called St Enda's House marks the site of his monastery, in the vicinity of which 120 saints are said to be buried. Enda trained many of the early saints; one of his pupils, St Ciarán of Clonmacnois, has a church and holy well dedicated to him on the island. St Brendan reputedly visited Enda here before setting out on his epic voyage. Also on Inishmore is an oratory, Teampull Benén, dedicated to St Patrick's disciple Benignus, and the grave of St Brecán, who renounced his life as a soldier and converted a pagan sanctuary here into a hermitage.

Each year on 14 June there is a pilgrimage to the smallest Aran Island of Inisheer. This is the feast of St Caomhán, who may have been the brother of Kevin of Glendalough. The roofless church is often filled with sand and usually has to be cleaned afresh for the occasion. The Aran Islands are also called the Islands of the Saints.

It is easy to imagine why the mild and fertile Isles of Scilly, also known as the Fortunate Islands, to the south-west of Land's End, were regarded as a heavenly land. The Abbey Gardens on Tresco have a feel of the Garden of Eden about them still. Avalon or Glasinnis were the Celtic names for the islands. Remains of early Celtic Christian chapels have been found on most of the larger islands and on St Helen's there was once a settlement similar to that on Skellig Michael.

The Celts had a very positive attitude towards death and dying, believing

*Opposite:* Penmon Priory and St Seriol's Well on Anglesey, St Michael weighing the souls of the dead, and the Old Man of Gugh, Isles of Scilly.

strongly in the Otherworld, and living with it as a daily reality. They saw death as a transition from one state to another in the context of a long and continuing life. In other words, eternal life was already being experienced and part of that was to live on the earthly plane for a time. Many meaningful rituals surrounded the death process. For instance, in Scotland a prayer called the "Soul Peace" or "Soul Leading" was intoned over a departing person by a soul-friend, usually someone very close to them. During the incantation the sign of the cross would be made with the right thumb on the lips of the dying one. In the mind of the Celtic Christians, it was St Michael who weighed the soul in his scales at death and prepared the way for it to enter the Kingdom of Heaven.

> *And may the strong Michael, high king of the angels,*
> *Be preparing the path before this soul, O God.*
> > *Amen.*
> *Oh! The strong Michael in peace with thee, soul,*
> *And preparing for thee the way to the kingdom of the Son of God.*
> > *Amen.*

from the *Carmina Gadelica* (i, 117)

The Celtic year has come full circle and we stand once again at the gateway to the new year, when the opportunity for new beginnings and for spiritual rebirth is offered to us. We can die to the old and be reborn to new life.

> *Death with oil,*
> *Death with joy,*
> *Death with light,*
> *Death with gladness,*
> > *Death with penitence.*
>
> *Death without pain,*
> *Death without fear,*
> *Death without death,*
> *Death without horror,*
> > *Death without grieving.*

> *May the seven angels of the Holy Spirit*
> > *And the two guardian angels*
> *Shield me this night and every night*
> > *Till light and dawn shall come;*
>
> > *Shield me this night and every night*
> > *Till light and dawn shall come.*

from the *Carmina Gadelica* (iii, 393)

# · THE · KINGDOM ·
## · OF · HEAVEN ·

*Blessed are the poor in spirit,*
*for theirs is the kingdom of heaven.*

Gospel of St Matthew (ch. 5, v. 3)

*W*HEN we feel content and at peace within ourselves, we are experiencing the Kingdom of Heaven and its deep joy. We are living in the present moment and not dwelling on the past or considering the future. This harmonious state of grace doesn't arise from a struggle; it has been created for us as children of God and it is our natural home. We relax with the knowledge that all things are held perfectly in the hand of God.

It doesn't depend on us achieving or acquiring, for often we still feel empty when we have gained something we have longed for, because we then move on to wanting the next thing we think will make us happy. Also, it doesn't depend on circumstances changing; it is open to us now.

True joy springs from aligning ourselves with the divine mind: that is, doing God's will, in more traditional Christian language. Not doing it is a denial of our true selves and a triumph of the ego. The quiet, remote Celtic places help us to recognize this still, restful centre within ourselves as deep calls to deep.

One of the hallmarks of the Celtic saints was their recognition of the immanence of the Kingdom and their ability to live in it daily. Our lower ego nature tells us not to be content with what is, but the saints teach us to relax, let go and let the order of the universe flow through us. We learn to give thanks constantly for the present moment and to be satisfied. This dwelling in the Kingdom of Heaven gives us an amazing freedom. We let go of judgements and preconceptions and know that all is well and moving towards healing.

We slowly learn to allow things to be as they are. We do not need to make things happen, but rather we allow their coming. What people say and do cannot make us unhappy at a deep level, for our joy is a constant state to be entered into at will. It is unchanging and exists beyond appearances.

Part of any pilgrim's task is to carry on the sanctification of the holy sites, but the underlying purpose of pilgrimage is to heal the soul and to find again the path that enables us to grow towards wholeness. It is time set aside in a place set apart when we can consider and reconsider without busyness. It should add depth and meaning to life.

In the Celtic tree calendar this short thirteenth month of three days is ruled by the elder, a tree of regeneration, of rebirth in the cycle of life and death. Letting go of the old is always balanced by the birth of the new and so it is a good symbol to have at the end of the year leading into the Celtic new year, which begins on the evening of 31 October.

My soul's desire is to enter the gates of heaven, and to gaze upon the light that shines for ever.     Amen.

from the *Carmina Gadelica*

Carved stone from the Shetlands showing four priests wearing hooded cloaks and carrying book satchels.

Spiral of Life, based on
*The Book of Kells*.

# INDEX